when
objects
talk

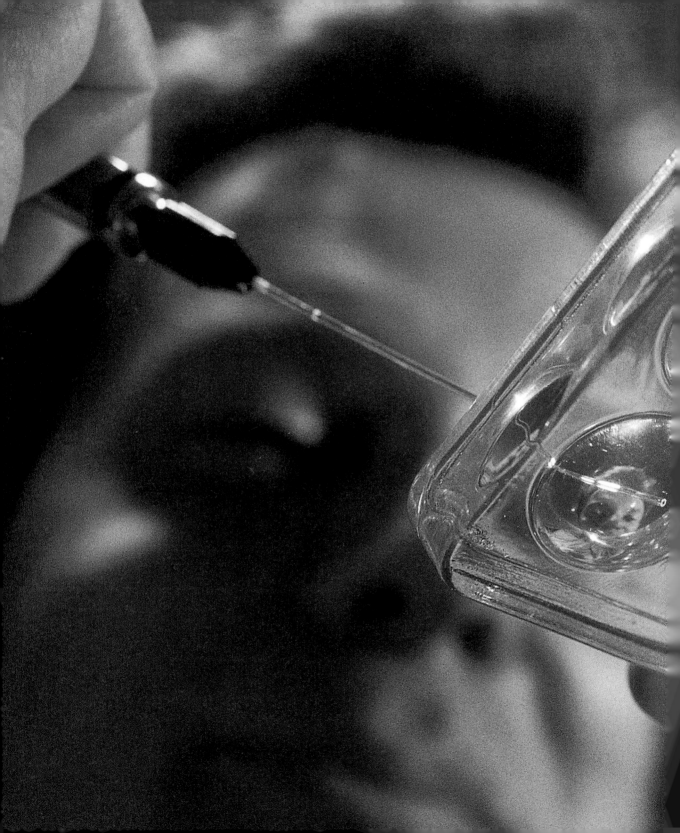

when objects talk

Solving a Crime with Science

Mark P. Friedlander Jr. and
Terry M. Phillips, Ph.D., D.Sc.

LERNER PUBLICATIONS COMPANY
MINNEAPOLIS

This book is dedicated to Karen, Mark, Helen, Susan, Rex, Todd, Andrew, Lisa, and Thomas.

Special thanks to Drs. George Mushrush and Douglas Mose at George Mason University, Fairfax, Virginia, who helped solve a crime; James Cowden, retired detective, Fairfax County Police, who kept us on target; and Lee Engfer, editor, and Melissa Warden, production editor, who made the manuscript work.

Lerner Publications Company
A division of Lerner Publishing Group
241 First Avenue North
Minneapolis, MN 55401 U.S.A.

Website address: www.lernerbooks.com

Library of Congress Cataloging-in-Publication Data

Friedlander, Mark P.
    When objects talk : solving a crime with science / by Mark P. Friedlander, Jr.,
    and Terry M. Phillips.
        p.   cm.
    Includes bibliographical references and index.
    ISBN: 0-8225-0649-1 (lib. bdg. : alk. paper)
    1. Criminal investigation—Juvenile literature. 2. Forensic sciences—Juvenile literature.
[1. Forensic sciences. 2. Criminal investigation.] I. Phillips, Terry M. II. Title.
HV8073.8 .F76 2001
363.25—dc21   00-010247

Manufactured in the United States of America
2 3 4 5 6 7 – JR – 08 07 06 05 04 03

CONTENTS

Introduction / 7

[1] The Crime: Bloodstain Patterns / 15

[2] Paper Trail: Document Examination / 23

[3] The Body Speaks: The Autopsy / 31

[4] Picking up Clues:
Particle Analysis / 41

[5] Dirt Talks: Forensic Geochemistry / 53

[6] Skull and Bones:
Forensic Anthropology / 61

[7] Assembling the Facts:
Probable Cause / 71

[8] Sound Evidence:
Audio Reconstruction / 79

[9] Unique Traces: Fingerprinting and
DNA Testing / 85

[10] Closing In: Ballistics / 97

Conclusion: Solving the Crime / 105

Glossary / 114
Further Reading / 117
Index / 118

INTRODUCTION

You have watched the scene on television. Whether it was on a newscast or a crime show, the procedure was the same. There has been a murder—a homicide, in police lingo. The police arrive, and officers quickly encircle the area with yellow police-line tape. No one is allowed to touch anything. Then the crime investigation team shows up.

A photographer takes pictures of the crime scene. An investigator makes sketches and takes measurements. Others search for clues—large, small, and minute. The investigators gather items and place them in containers and plastic bags. Samples of blood or other fluids are taken. Surfaces are dusted for fingerprints. The medical examiner checks the murder victim's body, and then it is removed to the morgue for an autopsy.

When newspaper and television reporters press for answers, a police spokesperson usually gives some minimal information, saying, "We have to wait for the autopsy and the lab reports."

And that is where our book begins. While the detectives look for clues, question witnesses, and try to develop a theory about who committed the crime, the men and women in the crime laboratories begin their work. They are forensic scientists.

The word *forensic* means "relating to or concerning the law." Forensic science means using the tools of scientific study in law enforcement and court cases. Forensic pathology, forensic toxicology, and forensic anthropology are all branches of forensic science.

To preserve evidence, police investigators set off the crime scene with yellow tape. No one else is allowed within the crime area.

Traditionally, forensic scientists have examined tiny particles of materials like glass, paint, fabric, and hair to determine if these particles can link a suspect to the crime scene. The jagged edges of a tiny piece of glass found embedded in the sole of a shoe worn by a suspect may exactly match a piece of broken mirror in the victim's home.

The world's first crime laboratory was established in 1910 by a French criminologist named Edmond Locard. Locard's lab consisted of a microscope, a spectroscope (an instrument for examining light, or optical spectra), and basic chemistry materials, all stuffed into two attic rooms above the local courthouse in Lyons, France. In later years, the lab grew and became known as the Lyons Police Laboratory. Locard's contribution to forensic science was a theory he developed called the "exchange principle."

Locard believed that when two objects or people come in contact with each other, there is an exchange of material between them. Tiny particles from each object are transferred to the other. Thus, particles move from the criminal to the victim or the crime scene, and vice versa. These particles can help prove that a criminal was at the crime scene or interacted with the victim. A few strands of a victim's hair found on the seat of a criminal's car may be enough to convict someone.

Several years after Locard set up his crime lab, he faced the challenging case of a young woman who had been strangled to death. Her boyfriend was the prime suspect, but he claimed to have been visiting friends that evening at a location far from the crime scene. Locard visited the suspect at the local jail and obtained scrapings from under his fingernails. Examining the scrapings under a microscope, Locard found particles of skin mixed with a pink dust. When he analyzed

A forensic expert carefully examines a murder scene.

the dust chemically, he learned that it was a mixture of chemicals, including a dye known as Venetian red. An inquiry at the local pharmacy revealed that the victim's face powder was specially prepared for her and contained all of the chemicals found under her boyfriend's nails, including Venetian red dye. Confronted with this evidence, the boyfriend confessed. The exchange principle worked.

That's why forensic scientists carefully collect even the smallest particles found at a crime scene. When the items arrive at the crime laboratory, they are carefully analyzed. This work involves many branches of science, including chemistry, biology, geology, metallurgy, physics, entomology, anthropology, serology, and pathology. Pathology is the study of disease and disease processes. Forensic pathology refers to the medical examination of human bodies affected by crime.

Principal Players in the Criminal Justice System

Many popular TV programs involve police and the courts. In real life as well as fictional stories, a number of "characters" have a role in bringing a criminal to justice for committing a crime.

• **Homicide detectives** are the lead law enforcement officers in charge of investigating a murder. The police officers who initially discover or respond to the homicide assist the homicide detectives in their investigation.

• The **coroner** and the **medical examiner** are sometimes the same person, especially in small towns and rural communities, but their functions are a little different. The medical examiner must have a medical degree (M.D.) and four years in residency in pathology (residency is a period of advanced training after graduation), followed by several more years of special training as a forensic pathologist. A pathologist may become a forensic pathologist or a hospital pathologist. Hospital pathologists examine bodies to look for natural diseases, while forensic pathologists deal with unnatural deaths, including murders, suicides, and accidents.

A coroner, on the other hand, is a government official, either elected or appointed, depending on local laws. A coroner is not necessarily a physician or a trained forensic pathologist, although in most places, the coroner is required to be a doctor. While investigating a possible homicide; the coroner can convene a "coroner's inquest," an inquiry in which witnesses give testimony, investigators present evidence, and the coroner or a jury decides if there is probable cause to believe that the dead person was murdered.

• Many different **forensic specialists** examine evidence (identified in parentheses below) and testify in court. These specialists include hematologists (blood), anthropologists (bones), toxicologists (drugs and poisons), entomologists (insects), odontologists (teeth), and psychiatrists (mental health).

• The **prosecuting attorney** is sometimes called the district attorney, state's attorney, or commonwealth attorney. The prosecuting attorney represents the government—federal, state, county, or city—in prosecuting, or trying, criminal cases. Usually the prosecuting attorney is a lawyer licensed in the state. Some prosecutors are appointed to their office, but they are usually elected officials. The prosecutor determines whether someone should be prosecuted for a crime and decides what crimes will be charged against the person.

• A **judge** is an appointed or elected official. Federal judges are appointed by the president and confirmed by the Senate. A judge presides over a court of justice and has judicial powers established by law. A **magistrate** has more limited powers. These differ from place to place, but often include the power to issue a warrant for the arrest of a person charged with a crime. The term *judicial officer* covers both judges and magistrates.

• There are two types of **juries.** The one most often seen on television programs is the "petit jury." This is a group of twelve people (or fewer in some civil cases) who together determine the guilt or innocence of the **defendant**—the person charged with committing a crime. In most states, the judge determines the sentence, or punishment, after the jury has determined guilt, but in some states the jury also sets the sentence.

The other type of jury is the "grand jury." Grand juries make official inquiries into crimes committed within their county or city. Usually a grand jury has between twelve and twenty-three members. The group meets from time to time to hear evidence produced by a prosecuting attorney or obtained by issuing subpoenas on their own initiative. A subpoena is a court order requiring someone to appear in court.

If a grand jury decides there is enough evidence to believe that a crime has been committed, they issue an indictment, a document stating the details of the crime with which a person is charged. The indicted person is then arrested and brought into the judicial system to stand trial.

When scientists study particles and other types of evidence, they discover important clues that help solve crimes. In other words, the objects "talk."

SCIENCE AND THE LAW

For a forensic scientist's work to be valuable in solving crimes, the laboratory findings must be able to be used in a courtroom at the criminal trial. If there is a mistake in the way items are collected, how they are cared for in transit or in storage, or in testing, the findings will not be considered admissible evidence—evidence that can be presented in court. Suppose a police detective takes an overturned glass from a crime scene, and the suspect's fingerprints are found on the glass. Detectives determine that there would be no reason for the suspect's prints to be on that glass unless he was at the scene when the crime was committed. This fact might help a jury conclude that the suspect was responsible for the crime.

However, if no one can explain where the glass was found or prove that it was at the crime scene, then the judge would likely declare the glass inadmissible evidence. As a result, the jury would never hear about the glass, and the criminal might go free.

This is why officers and detectives at a crime scene must be very careful to identify and label each item they gather. They record exactly who has handled the item at any time, a procedure called "chain of custody." This process ensures that, at the trial, the prosecuting attorney will be able to establish several facts: (1) only proper law enforcement officers collected, identified, labeled, and cataloged the evidence; (2) the evidence was properly protected, usually in a police property room, locked file cabinet, evidence locker, or vault; (3) everyone who handled the item can be identified; (4) no one had the opportunity to substitute a different item or tamper with the evidence; and (5) the appropriate tests were performed on the item of evidence traced through this chain of custody.

At the trial, witnesses testify about how and when they handled the evidence to demonstrate the chain of custody. Then forensic experts testify about the equipment and methods they used in performing tests and give their opinion on the meaning of the results.

Not all forensic science is aimed at solving murder cases. Forensic scientists help solve all manner of crimes, including arson, rape, robbery, burglary, theft, forgery, and fraud. Forensic scientists work on civil cases as well as criminal cases. In criminal law, the government (federal, state, and local) prosecutes and punishes people who harm the public safety. In civil cases, individuals seek compensation for private wrongs. A driver who runs a red light and smashes into someone else's car has committed the crime of driving recklessly. As a criminal case, the reckless driver can be prosecuted and punished by the government for harming the public safety. At the same time, the person whose car was hit can sue the driver in a civil court for the costs of the damage done to the car and any injuries its passengers suffered. Civil court cases that might require the services of forensic scientists include automobile, train, and airplane accidents, machinery and product failures, and building collapses. This book discusses forensic science as it relates to solving criminal cases, particularly murder.

Chapter One

THE CRIME:
BLOODSTAIN PATTERNS

THE CASE

Ann Marlboro, her husband, Tim, and their seven-year-old son, Timmy Jr., live in a two-story brick house in Annandale, a comfortable suburban community in Fairfax County, Virginia, south of Washington, D.C. The lawn is neat, but recent rains have left the grass a little long. An elderly neighbor, who spends part of her time watching the comings and goings of her neighbors and much of the rest of her time gossiping about what she sees, has noticed that the Marlboros' house has been unusually quiet. For several days, no one has gone in or out of the house. She calls the police to explain her concern.

"Perhaps they're just out of town," suggests the police operator.

"No," she says, "if they'd gone away, they'd have asked me to take in their newspapers and mail. They're piled by the front door."

Two police officers come to the house. When no one answers the door, they enter through an unlocked door and search the house. On the floor of the master bedroom, they discover the bloody body of a woman. Ann Marlboro has been brutally murdered! There is no sign of Tim or little Timmy.

Bloodstains provide valuable evidence for the forensic investigator.

Officers immediately set up a line of yellow crime-scene tape around the house and call the homicide detectives. The murder investigation has begun.

Detective Elizabeth Sullivan, a twelve-year veteran of the police force, is in charge. She is a lean, angular woman with bright red hair who walks in a perpetual slouch from spending a lifetime trying to minimize her six-foot-one-inch height. Her partner, Detective Mario Vasquez, is a short, rotund man with a round face, thick black hair, and dark-rimmed glasses. He has recently risen from the ranks of the police to become a detective.

While a police photographer snaps pictures of the victim and the room, Sullivan points to blood splatters on the walls and furniture. Without saying a word, Vasquez nods and begins measuring the distances between the splatters. Sullivan and Vasquez are both aware that bloodstain patterns can tell a vivid story of the events that unfolded during a murder. Interpreting these patterns can be critical in solving the crime.

BLOODSTAIN PATTERNS

The way a drop of blood hits the ground, a wall, or another surface depends on many factors, such as how far it fell and which direction it came from. By analyzing bloodstain patterns, investigators gain many clues about a crime. A drop of blood falling straight down from a cut will leave a perfectly round splat, for example, while blood that is projected becomes elongated as it strikes a surface. The rounder a projection stain, the shorter the distance the blood traveled. More oval and elongated projection stains indicate that the blood traveled farther.

Bloodstains have certain "edge characteristics" that indicate the direction the blood traveled. In a stain that is shaped like a

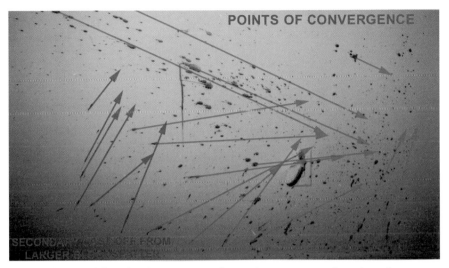

POINTS OF CONVERGENCE

SECONDARY CAST-OFF FROM
LARGER BLOOD SPATTER

By analyzing bloodstain patterns, investigators can pinpoint the location of the victim at the moment of the attack.

teardrop, the narrow tip points in the direction from which the blood came. If there is a series of stains with elongated edges, a direction can be determined for each stain. All of the paths for one series can be traced or projected back to a single "point of convergence." This is where the wound occurred. If there are several points of convergence at a crime scene, the victim was probably running or walking while bleeding.

In the past, crime investigators located the point of convergence by stretching a piece of string from each blood splat in the direction that the splatter suggested the blood traveled. The place where the strings intersected indicated the location of the victim at the moment of the attack. Investigators can now use a computer program called *No More Strings,* which simulates a three-dimensional view of a crime scene using information taken from blood splatters.

Blood patterns also show whether the blood was coming from a vein or an artery. Blood from an artery pumps in rhythmic jets as the victim's heart beats, while blood from a vein moves in a slow, steady flow. Blood gushing from an artery leaves a pattern of large stains on the ground and a downward flow on walls.

If someone is attacked with a knife or a blunt instrument such as a hammer or pipe, the blood leaves a telltale pattern on nearby walls or ceilings. The blood splatters will show the arc, or swing, that the knife or club made as the attacker struck. By measuring the angles of the splatters and their point of convergence, an investigator can locate the position of the attacker.

Sometimes a bloodstain pattern gets wiped by a person or object during the course of the crime. Then a secondary pattern appears, with edges that feather away from the stain in the direction of the wipe. Specialists can tell whether a hand, foot, shoe, or hair touched a blood splat. Each of these leaves a characteristic mark.

Analyzing bloodstains and other fluid patterns is a forensic specialty that requires extensive training and experience. During the investigation, a photographer takes careful color photographs of the crime scene to show the overall bloodstain patterns as well as each individual drop or splatter. Often the photographer uses special film to locate blood splatters that are not visible to the naked eye. To record bloodstains consistently and accurately, all photographs are taken from an exact 90-degree angle. This work must be done before blood samples are taken for tests.

Some blood splatters are visible and obvious, but others are not easily seen. Someone may have tried to wipe the blood away, or the drops or traces of blood may be very small. If investigators suspect that "invisible" bloodstains are in an area, they apply a chemical known as Luminol. Any blood then shows up in darkness as a bluish-white reflection from an ultraviolet (UV) light, sometimes called a "Woods lamp." Further tests are then performed to make sure that the Luminol is not reacting with paints or cleaning fluids that can cause the same reaction.

One edge of a bloodstain may be thicker than the rest of the stain. If a drop of blood strikes the side of a chair and runs downward, the stain will be thicker at the bottom than at the top because of the pull of gravity. If the splatter is thicker at the side than at the bottom, this suggests that the chair was knocked over during the event, then righted later.

BLOOD TESTING

The science of blood testing is known as forensic serology. To determine if blood found on a victim or at a crime scene is from a suspect, blood samples are tested. First, the blood is tested to see if it is human. If it is, it is classified according to blood type. All humans have one of four types of blood—A, B, AB, or O. The types are based on the presence or absence of two antigens (substances that cause an immune response), A and B. If you're type AB, your blood would test positive for both the A and B antigens. Type O blood contains neither A nor B.

Of course, millions of people have each blood type, so that test alone is not enough to identify blood and prove a suspect's guilt. But blood also contains a number of enzymes and proteins known as genetic markers. These markers differ from person to person, and labs can identify them in a blood sample. Serologists test for about a dozen different markers, and each test narrows the possibilities of whose blood it could be. For example, the enzyme phosphoglucomutase, or PGM, is found in everyone's blood, but at least ten different types of PGM have been identified. So while two people may have the same blood type, they are much less likely to have the same blood type *and* the same PGM type. If three or four of the same genetic markers are found in each of two blood samples, the chance that the samples are from different people is about one million to one. Blood testing is about 99 percent accurate.

THE CASE

In the master bedroom of the Marlboro house, Sullivan kneels down to examine the chair while Vasquez walks around the room, surveying the scene. "Oh, man," he says, "if these walls could talk, what a story they could tell us."

Sullivan rises from her position next to the chair. She smiles. "Ah, Vasquez, but they can. The objects in this room can talk. When the people at the lab are done, this room will tell us a lot.

"But we don't need to wait for the lab reports," she adds. "We can already tell that this chair has been moved."

"How's that?"

"For one thing, it's not sitting on the four leg indentations in the carpet. And look at this blood splatter pattern. It doesn't fit with its location on the chair."

Vasquez kneels beside the chair and examines it closely. He removes his glasses, wipes them with the end of his necktie, and looks again. "You're right, Sullivan. The thickened edge is facing back, toward the side of the chair, not downward, even though the chair is sitting upright."

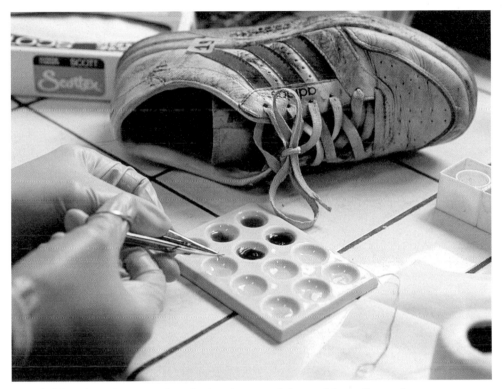

A blood typing tray (agglutination tray) is used by a forensic hematologist to identify blood types.

"Yes. That chair was on its side when the drop of blood struck it. As the blood dried, it became thicker on the edge. But we didn't find the chair on its side. That means it was knocked over during the murder and set upright afterward. And there's another sign of a struggle—the lightbulb in the lamp is broken."

Vasquez nods.

They both look around the room again. That's when Vasquez notices a crumpled piece of paper on the floor, sticking out from underneath the bed.

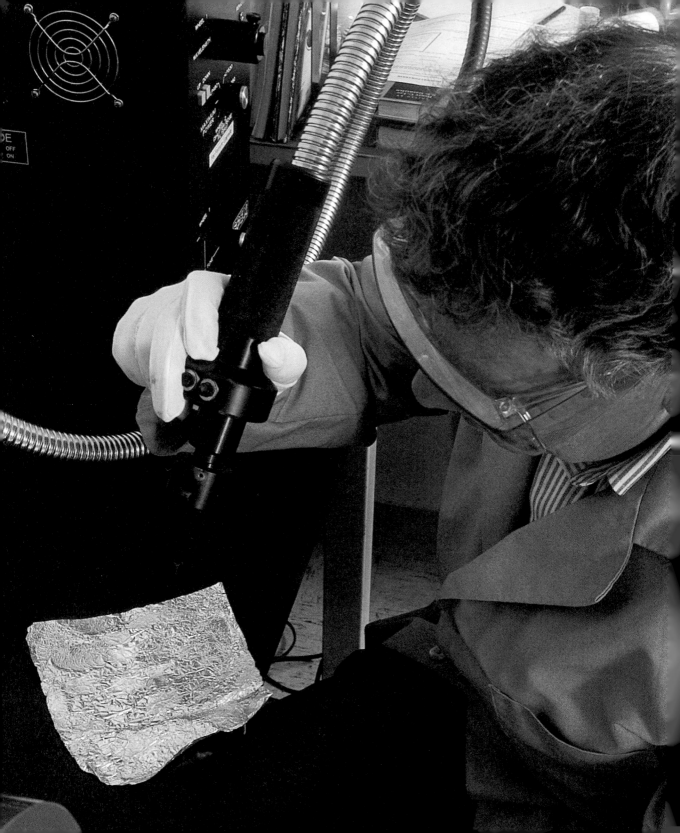

Chapter Two

PAPER TRAIL:
DOCUMENT EXAMINATION

THE CASE

Vasquez dons a pair of lightweight latex gloves so that he will not mar any fingerprints or leave his own on the piece of paper. Then he reaches under the bed to retrieve the crumpled paper. He walks over to Sullivan and carefully uncrumples the single sheet of pink paper, touching only the edges.

Just then, a police officer approaches. "Background," he says, reading from his notepad. "The victim is Ann Marlboro, age thirty-two, married to Timothy Marlboro, age forty. They have one child, Tim Jr., age seven. Husband and son have been in Ohio for the last four days. He's a clothing salesman in Reston, and Ann is a book-keeper at Selma Paint and Supply in Fairfax."

"Has he been contacted?"

"Yes," says the officer. "He'll be flying in on the first available plane."

"Good. We'll want to talk to him the minute he arrives," Sullivan says, taking notes.

For a moment, she thinks about the woman's son and shakes her head sadly. Looking back at the body on the floor, she does a double take. "The murderer was a man!" she announces.

Fingerprints can be revealed by a number of methods, including subjecting an object to ultraviolet light.

"What?"

"And I'll bet there are some dirt particles in this carpet that will tell us where the guy was just before the murder."

"Please explain," Vasquez says in amazement.

"Her shoes."

Vasquez looks at the woman's shoes. They are expensive, low-heeled brown pumps, only slightly worn.

Sullivan explains, "Her shoes are brown. The lady is dressed in a black skirt and white blouse with a red scarf. No woman would wear brown shoes with black, white, and red. I bet her killer noticed something on her shoes that he feared would give him away. He must have removed the shoes she was wearing, gone into her closet, and put a clean pair of shoes on her feet. But he didn't notice the lack of color coordination." Sullivan gently touches her partner's shoulder. "No woman, even a murderess, would have made that mistake.

"After the medical examiner is finished, we'll have this carpet scraped and vacuumed and the closet doorknob dusted for prints. In the meantime, let's take a look at the paper you found."

"It's an invoice," he says, holding up a business invoice that reads:

Selma Paint and Supply Company
445400 Main Street
Fairfax, Virginia 22302
Phone 703-893-9600

Invoice Number A16482

Ship to: **Wellington Hardware and Supply**
                Route 29
                Ruckersville, Virginia

10 Gal. Bright White Exterior
        @ $15.00 per gal. = $150.00

Vasquez wrinkles his forehead. "What does paint have to do with this crime?"

"Seems like an ordinary invoice," Sullivan says. "Let's let the lab take a look."

"OK, I'll bag it."

Many crimes involve paper and writing. Crimes such as forgery, fraud, and counterfeiting are committed on paper. A paper associated with a crime is called a "questioned document." The document may be handwritten, typewritten, or printed. It is usually on paper, but it can also be on a wall, clothing, or even a body. The document is "questioned" because investigators are not sure if it is genuine or falsified. Has the document been altered, counterfeited, or forged? Whose handwriting is it?

But a questioned document can also reveal many clues that have nothing to do with forgery. Forensic scientists look at many different parts of a document—not just what's written on the paper, but also how it was handled, what evidence remains on it, and the chemical makeup of the paper itself. Because many clues are too small to be seen with the naked eye or even a magnifying glass, the microscope is an essential tool in a crime laboratory.

First, scientists check a document for fingerprints. They also look for identifying marks from a typewriter, computer printer, fax machine, or photocopy machine. Slight variations in the imprint of a typewriter key or printer head can be seen under a microscope. These variations, such as a tiny chip in the imprint of an "o," can connect the questioned document to a specific typewriter. Because many printers, fax machines, and photocopiers have minute defects in the grippers and blades used to hold and cut paper, investigators can often match a piece of paper to the specific machine on which it was produced. Investigators also notice any paper tears or staple marks.

Ink also provides a wealth of information. The colored part of the ink, called the pigment, remains on the surface of the paper. But a chemical called a solvent, which carries the pigment, soaks into the fibers of the paper. If the writing has been erased from a document, removing the pigment, forensic examiners can make the solvent visible by using ultraviolet or infrared lights and cameras fitted with various filters. Ultraviolet and infrared light are parts of the light spectrum that are not visible to the eye. Sometimes they can reveal details that cannot be seen by the naked eye—so that the invisible becomes visible.

Using these techniques, the forensic scientist can identify letters or numbers that have been added to or subtracted from a document. Say a forger takes a check written to him for $4 and adds the word "hundred" to the four and "00" after the 4 to increase the amount of the check to $400. This alteration might not be detectable to the naked eye, but a forensic examiner can detect the forgery using a camera with special filters and different kinds of light.

If a person writes on a pad of paper with a pencil or a ballpoint pen, the sheet of paper underneath the top sheet may have indentations where the pen pressed down. These indentations are often not visible. But shining a flashlight at an angle across the document can reveal the indentations of the words. It's also possible to bring out these indentations by brushing a sheet of paper lightly with a pencil, but forensic scientists prefer to use light to avoid tampering with the document.

Another device scientists use to bring out invisible indentations on paper is the electrostatic detection apparatus. The piece of paper is placed on a sheet of glass that rests on top of a

Ink from a printed item can be examined under a microscope to help trace the item to the machine that produced it.

brass plate. The document is then covered with a sheet of very thin, clear plastic. A vacuum holds the glass and the plastic tightly together. Then the brass plate is electrically charged, and black toner (the type used in copy machines) is dusted over the plastic sheet. The toner responds to the electric charge by filling in or highlighting the indentations. The now-visible writing can be photographed and preserved for use in court.

Crime laboratories also examine the chemical content of inks. Inks are composed of a mixture of dyes. Since 1969, many ink manufacturers have added a chemical identifier to their inks, so they can be easily identified. Examiners can identify the manufacturer and manufacturing date with great accuracy. To analyze ink dyes, scientists use a process called chromatography. In chromatography, solvent chemicals (chemicals that dissolve other specific chemicals) are used to extract and separate different components of the ink. The chemical content of ink can reveal alterations made in a document, such as writing added with a different pen or at a later time.

Paper, too, can be identified by its contents. Amazingly, paper that has been soaked, crumpled, or even burned can often be restored for examination. If the paper is wet, it is dried in a freezer. A burned piece of paper that has not crumbled into ashes can be placed in an envelope of very thin polyester film for easy handling and then examined under infrared light to bring out the inks. A chemical called parylene is used to give badly crumpled paper extra strength so that it can be uncrumpled and read.

Handwriting identification often captures the most attention. But handwriting identification and comparison are a very inexact science. Even though everyone's handwriting is different, no one writes his or her name exactly the same way twice. If the authenticity of a handwriting sample is challenged in court, the examiner collects samples of the suspect's handwriting from approximately the same time as the suspected forgery for comparison. If these are not available, the suspect will be asked to write the same words in front of a law enforcement officer or forensic examiner using the same type of paper and pencil or pen as was used for the suspected forgery.

Advanced computer programs are useful tools in handwriting and printing identification.

These handwriting samples are called exemplars. A person's handwriting, including his or her printing, contains many identifiable characteristics, such as the way the person writes parts of letters and the place where the pen or pencil first touches the paper or leaves the paper when a particular letter or number is written. These traits become even more apparent when the exemplars are examined under a microscope or with a special computer program. People who specialize in handwriting comparison usually have many years of experience in this forensic specialty.

THE CASE

Later, Detectives Sullivan and Vasquez are seated at their desks when they receive a call from the crime lab. Sullivan leans toward the phone to pick it up. "Sullivan here."

"Hi Sully," says the lab technician. "The only prints on that invoice belong to the subject. But there's something strange. One of the invoice numbers was added at a later date."

"How's that?"

"The original invoice number was A1648. Under the microscope we saw that the 2 was added later to make the number A16482. A skilled likeness to the other numbers—hard to detect. The ink is from a different source. I would say that the 2 was added much later." He pauses. "Why someone would want to forge an extra number on an invoice I'll leave to you guys. See ya."

"Well," says Sullivan after reporting the information to Vasquez, "as soon as we have the autopsy report, we'll need to pay a visit to Selma Paint and Supply Company."

Chapter Three

THE BODY SPEAKS:
THE AUTOPSY

THE C A SE

The next call Sullivan gets is from Anne Riley, the medical examiner. "Which one of you is joining me for the autopsy?" Riley asks.

Sullivan turns to her partner. "You go ahead, Vasquez. I promised Amy I'd be there for her ballet class."

"OK," replies Vasquez. "I've never been at an autopsy anyway. It'll be a good experience."

Sullivan raises her eyebrows. "It certainly will be an experience," she says.

An autopsy is the medical examination of a dead body. Autopsies may be done at a hospital if doctors cannot determine a patient's cause of death. A *medicolegal* autopsy is performed when the death is violent, unexpected, or suspicious. The medical examiner or coroner investigates not only murders, but also accidents or suicides. During the autopsy, the examiner determines:

- the age and sex of the victim
- the time of death
- the cause of death (e.g., disease, drowning, poisoning)
- the manner of death (suicide, homicide, accident, unknown)

Toe tags differentiate the bodies in a morgue from one another.

[31]

The autopsy can provide many clues that will aid detectives in finding the killer or killers. A police representative or detective who was at the crime scene usually attends the autopsy.

The medical examiner performs the autopsy at the morgue, a local facility where dead people can be examined and kept until they are identified and removed for burial. But the examiner's work begins at the crime scene. There, he or she performs an initial examination of the body, noting and photographing external, visible conditions. The body temperature must be recorded to help determine the time of death—a body cools at a predictable rate after death. Often the medical examiner wraps the victim's hands in plastic bags to allow for a later examination of microscopic fibers, hairs, skin, or other material trapped under the fingernails. If the victim struggled with his or her attacker, blood or tiny particles from the attacker's clothing or skin may have lodged under the victim's fingernails. This material can offer clues to the killer's identity.

The body is then placed in a plastic body bag and transported to the morgue. At the morgue, the body is lifted onto a stainless steel examining table and removed from the bag. The medical examiner then begins the autopsy. As the examiner works, he or she reports the findings into an overhead microphone connected to a tape recorder. The examiner or an assistant also takes photographs at various points.

First the clothing is carefully removed. If necessary, this can be done at the murder site, but it usually happens at the morgue. The clothing, which may be wet from being outside or soaked with body fluids, is dried in a laboratory oven before being placed in specimen bags. Drying preserves any stains on the clothes, keeping them from spreading and contaminating other parts of the clothing. The forensic examiner

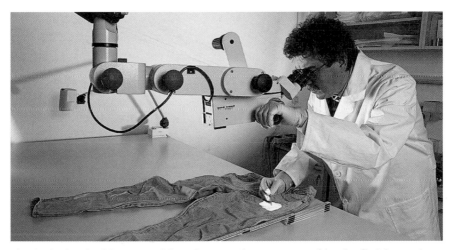

A victim's clothing provides clues such as traces of body fluids, stains, fibers, hair, and other particles.

draws conclusions about the crime based on the location of stains such as blood. The clothing is also searched for fibers, hair, and other particles. Often clothing is vacuumed to retrieve microscopic particles.

Once all the clothing has been removed, samples of the victim's blood are collected and stored, along with hairs from the head. The medical examiner checks the body for any distinguishing features, such as birthmarks or healed scar tissue. He or she also looks for recent marks such as bullet entry and exit wounds, stab wounds, blunt injury wounds, powder burns, scrapes, and scratches. A blunt injury is caused by an object that does not have a sharpened cutting edge. Wounds from these injuries appear as a crushed-in area rather than a cut or puncture. Powder burns result from close contact with a discharging gun. The burn is caused by the hot gases and gunpowder particles ejected from the barrel of a fired gun.

Next, all major body cavities—mouth, nostrils, throat, ears, eyes, genitals, and anus—are examined. The examiner takes a swab of body fluids such as saliva for later examination under the microscope. The body is then carefully weighed and measured. After this has been done, the plastic bags are removed from the hands. The material under the fingernails is collected, to be examined later.

Then the medical examiner is ready to begin the cutting part of the autopsy. The body is laid on its back with a support to slightly raise the head. Using a scalpel, the examiner carefully makes an incision in the form of a Y. The top of the Y starts at the shoulders, and the incisions come together just under the breastbone. Then the examiner cuts in a straight line down the

During autopsies, tissue samples from organs are preserved and stored for further study and for use as evidence at trials.

middle of the body to just above the pubic area. With a special bone-cutting tool, all of the ribs are cut apart. Then the ribs and the breastbone are removed, exposing the lungs and heart, which are removed, weighed, and dissected.

Next, the examiner cuts through the abdominal muscles to reach the internal organs in the lower part of the body. Usually the stomach, intestines, liver, kidneys, and spleen are removed for examination. Tissue samples from the organs are placed in a liquid preservative called formalin. The samples will be examined later under the microscope. The examiner looks for minor splits or rips in the abdominal muscles and membranes, which would suggest a blow to the stomach, and notes any punctures or cuts.

Finally, the medical examiner looks at the brain. This requires a second incision, from ear to ear around the back of the head. The scalp is temporarily peeled forward over the face to reveal the bones of the skull. To expose the brain, the skull is cut open with a special electric oscillating saw. The examiner first checks the brain for hemorrhages (large discharges of blood from the blood vessels) or blood clots, which could be caused by a blow to the head. Then he or she lifts the brain toward the back of the skull and cuts the optic tracts and spinal cord. The brain is removed, weighed, and examined. Some sections are taken for microscopic examination.

By studying the appearance of the victim and the condition of the organs, the medical examiner can usually determine the cause of death. For instance, mild bruising and tears in tissue may be self-inflicted, but major organ damage and ruptured blood vessels are usually caused by an accident or a homicide. Likewise, multiple knife wounds to the upper back would rule out suicide, since no one would be able to stab himself that way. Fluid in the lungs suggests death by drowning. Analysis of the stomach contents can tell examiners if the person died of poisoning or a drug overdose.

When the examiner's work is completed, an assistant replaces all the organs, moves the skin of the head back into place, and stitches up the body. The body is then washed with water and placed in the morgue freezer if further examination is needed, or in a refrigerator if the body is going to a funeral home.

THE CASE

Vasquez, cloaked in a pale green surgeon's gown, with a face mask and cap, stands next to Anne Riley, the medical examiner.

"The likely cause of death," says Riley, "is internal bleeding from a bullet wound. Looks like the pistol was fired at close range." She points to a hole in the chest surrounded by powder burns. "But there are also stab wounds, so we'll just take a good look."

Slowly and carefully, she examines the entire body, all the while making comments into an overhead microphone. When she reaches the hands, she removes the plastic bags. She looks closely at each hand and finger, removes the wedding ring, and scrapes under the fingernails, using a stainless steel spatula. She places the scrapings in plastic bags, notes which hand and finger each sample of material is from, and saves them for further examination.

"Now that I have completed the external examination, I'll do the incisions," Riley says. "Are you sure you want to watch this part?"

"Yes," answers Vasquez.

"OK." Riley lifts her scalpel and begins to cut.

After the first incision, Vasquez steps back, puts his hands to his mouth, and darts from the room.

Riley shakes her head. "Detective Vasquez has departed the examining room to respond to important police business," she says into the microphone. Then she adds to herself, "It always happens on the first time—with cops, medical students, and sometimes even doctors."

Later, when she finishes, she walks into the conference room where Vasquez is waiting.

"Sorry, Doc," he says.

Riley brushes aside the apology. "No problem. That happened to me, too, the first time. You get used to it after a while."

The two sit down and Riley turns to Vasquez. "Here's what I found," she says. "The initial examination of the body revealed a bullet wound to the chest and two deep stab wounds to the upper arm and shoulder. Based on the shape of the stab wounds, I'd say they were inflicted with a single-edge blade, eight or nine inches long. Probably a Bowie or hunting knife.

"Judging from the angle of the stab wound to the shoulder, which stopped when it hit the scapula, or shoulder blade, I would suspect that this was the first blow. The ragged edges of the wound indicate that the attacker wrenched the weapon out as the victim turned to face him. The second stab wound, on the arm, was likely the second attack, and the victim used her arm to defend herself."

Riley stops and walks to the counter to pour herself a cup of coffee from a dull, dented coffeepot. She nods an offer to Vasquez, who shakes his head. Returning to her chair, she continues. "There are no other stab or slash wounds, suggesting that the knife was knocked from the attacker's hands or that he abandoned the knife attack for some reason.

"Except for the knife wounds, the only other external injury was a bruise on the right temple. Killers will often feel the artery in the neck to see if their victim is really dead, so I didn't disturb the skin in that area. New techniques can sometimes detect fingerprints on skin. I'll have our fingerprint experts examine the skin for prints. We may even have to get help from the FBI lab.

"The temple area did show signs of trauma. On opening the skull, I found a huge hemorrhage, indicating that the victim received a blow to the head, possibly with a blunt instrument. Although the blow caused little external damage, I believe that the cranial injury was the cause of death. There were no other indications of brain injury or disease."

Vasquez is scribbling furiously in his notebook. "But what about the bullet wound?"

"Strangely, the gunshot to the chest did not kill her. She was shot after she was already dead."

Riley continues, "Although there is an entrance wound, I could not find an exit wound. When I opened her chest, I found the bullet lodged in the sternum, or breastbone. The bullet is a small caliber, possibly a .22 or .25. It was used to be sure she was dead, or to pretend that the gunshot killed her."

"Yeah," says Vasquez, "the .25 is used by many robbers. They call it the 'Saturday Night Special.'"

"Well, that's about it," Riley says with a tired smile.

Vasquez takes a few more notes, then says, "If I can summarize—the way you see it, the victim was attacked from the rear with a knife. She turned around and fought her attacker. Maybe she knocked the knife away. Then he struck a fatal blow to the side of her head with something heavy. She was either killed at that moment or fell unconscious and died shortly afterward. Meanwhile, the murderer fired a small-caliber weapon at close range, either to make sure she was dead or to make it look like the gunshot was the cause of death."

"Yes, exactly. The powder burns on her clothing show that." Riley stands up. "Finally, I should point out that the massive amount of blood at the crime scene came from the slight nick in the artery in the victim's forearm. That stab wound was not enough to kill her, but certainly enough to cover the place with blood."

"Thank you," says Vasquez.

As Riley reaches the door, she stops and turns. "Oh, by the way, there's one more thing."

"What?"

"Among the medicines the lab people collected at the victim's house was a prescription for her from a European pharmacy. It was for sleeping pills, but the Europeans still use barbiturates. I found barbiturates in her gastric fluid. This means that at some point before her death she took a sleeping pill. That could suggest that something was troubling her, but I may be reaching. Anyway, I thought I'd better mention it just in case."

Vasquez nods, opens the door, and hurries up the stairs and out into the sunshine, glad to be away from the morgue.

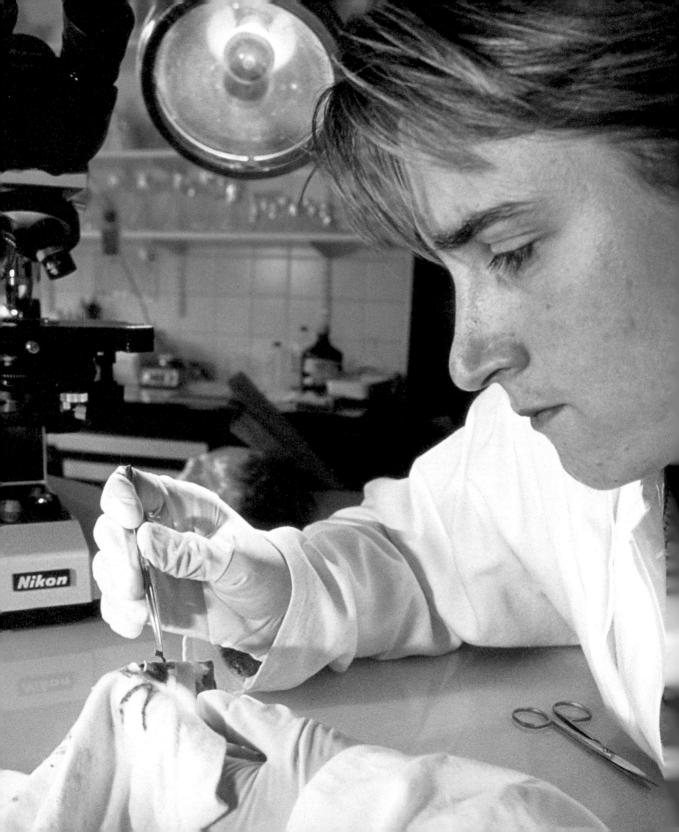

Chapter Four

PICKING UP CLUES:
PARTICLE ANALYSIS

THE CASE

When Vasquez reaches police headquarters, he finds Sullivan on the phone with the medical examiner. Sullivan turns on the speakerphone so Vasquez can listen to the conversation.

"Lab analysis found a variety of cellular material and some chemical residue under the subject's fingernails," Riley says. "Most of the cellular matter was cell debris, along with some dried blood cells. The blood was human and did not belong to the subject. All the material has been sent for DNA analysis."

"And the chemicals?" Both detectives take rapid notes. They will get a formal report later, but they don't want to wait.

"Very interesting," says Riley. "Analysis of the chemical residue reveals an abundance of lead. The folks at the lab also found other metallic trace elements. The composition of this material suggests that the attacker had some contact with lead-based paint."

"Hmm. Have you got anything else?"

"Nope. That's all for the moment." The phone clicks off.

Sullivan looks at Vasquez. "Now for our visit to the paint store."

Vasquez nods. "More pieces for the puzzle," he says as they grab their coats and head out the door.

Bloodstained fibers found on a victim's clothes are carefully collected and analyzed.

In a criminal investigation, even the tiniest particles found at the crime scene must be collected. These minute, even invisible, particles are referred to as microtraces.

Forensic experts use four main methods to collect particles:

(1) *Handpicking.* Investigators collect some particles by hand, using a sharp-pointed forceps, a strong light, and a powerful magnifying glass.

(2) *Taping.* Adhesive tape used for collecting particles must be sticky enough to catch the particles but thin enough and clear enough that it won't interfere with viewing particles through a microscope. Special tapes are manufactured for this purpose, although ordinary adhesive tape is often used.

(3) *Vacuuming.* Using a vacuum equipped with a clean filter, particles are vacuumed from a particular area, such as the victim's left pocket, a specific area in a room, or the backseat of the suspect's automobile. The filter used for that area is removed, sealed in a plastic bag, and labeled.

(4) *Washing.* If a stain or particle cannot be removed by handpicking, using adhesive tape, or vacuuming, then it must be washed out. This can be done with water or other solvents.

FIBERS

Fibers—pieces of thread from clothes or fabrics—represent valuable forensic evidence. Fibers may be found on a victim or suspect, at a crime scene or a suspect's home, or in a car. Because there are many different types of fibers, they can be used for identification. Some fibers come from plants, such as cotton, from animals, such as sheep's wool, or from insects, such as silk. Many fabrics are synthetic (created by humans), such as nylon and polyester.

Examining fibers under a microscope can often link them to a particular piece of clothing or a carpet from a house or car.

In a criminal investigation, fibers are usually gathered with clear adhesive tape or by vacuuming. Identifying a fiber as cotton or wool or nylon is just the beginning of the investigator's task. The quality of the fiber, the twists in the threads, and variations in color are also important. Were the threads dyed before being woven into cloth, or was the color applied afterward? Synthetic fibers often have a cross section that is particular to a specific manufacturer.

GLASS, PAINT, AND HAIR

Glass, paint, and hair are a few of the so-called trace items that can become valuable in identifying a criminal. Pieces of broken glass from a table lamp, a car headlight, or a broken window can lodge in a suspect's shoe soles or clothing. These fragments can then be traced to the source. Forensic scientists match the edges of glass fragments and determine the chemical and physical properties of each fragment. One test, called the refractive index, measures the angle at which light is bent when it travels through a piece of glass. A second test measures the density of the glass by placing samples in glass tubes containing liquids of different densities and seeing if the glass samples float.

Paint may be found at a crime scene as a smear or chip. Paint particles are also found on weapons, which may have rubbed against or struck a painted surface. Paint chips can be matched like a jigsaw puzzle to a chipped spot on a wall. Paint can also be analyzed directly to determine its chemical makeup.

Human hair is distinctive from animal hair, and hairs from the head, arms, legs, and other areas all have different features, such as length, color, shape, and root appearance. If a crime victim's hair is found on a suspect's clothing or belongings or in his car, this evidence can help link the suspect to the crime. Laboratory analysis of hair can reveal whether the person was using drugs or swallowed any other chemicals. Hair strands may also carry microscopic traces of blood, dust, fibers, or paint.

SOIL

Soil or dirt samples also provide valuable information about a crime. Forensic scientists can determine if soil found on a suspect's body or clothing matches soil found at the crime scene. Soil is typically made up of sand, clay, gravel, glass, and brick. It may also contain fertilizers and commercial chemicals, as well as organic matter such as animal droppings, seeds, decomposing leaves, and wood.

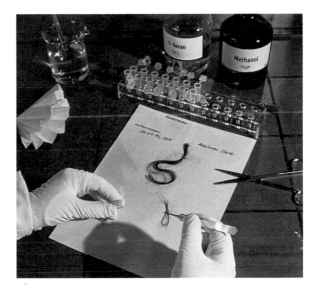

Hair samples can be used to detect drug use. As hair grows, it retains traces of chemicals that are produced when drugs are in the body. A suspect's drug use over time can be determined by examining different lengths of the suspect's hair.

In the laboratory, soil samples are examined under various types of light and the color is checked. Forensic scientists use a standard soil color chart to compare different soil samples. An investigator can match the color of a soil sample to a code on the chart and call a central agency, such as the Federal Bureau of Investigation (FBI), to find out the locations of soils matching that code.

After comparing the texture and color of soil samples, the investigator may wash them in an ultrasonic cleaner. High-frequency sound waves separate out minerals, glass particles, and brick fragments. These washed samples are then placed in bromoform, the common name for tribromomethane, a thick liquid in which lighter minerals float to the top and heavier ones sink to the bottom. If two samples separate in the same way, investigators can be fairly sure that the two samples came from the same place.

Once particles are collected, forensic specialists use many different instruments and procedures to examine them. One of the most important and basic tools for studying particles is the microscope.

THE WORLD OF MICROSCOPES

Anyone who has ever taken a science class is familiar with microscopes. These instruments produce enlarged images of small objects. There are many different types of microscopes. Optical microscopes use light and lenses to produce an enlarged image

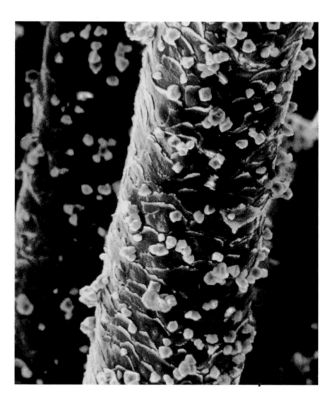

A strand of human hair retaining particles of shampoo, as viewed through a scanning electron microscope

of an object. Compound microscopes, optical microscopes with two or more lenses, are the standard laboratory instruments used in classrooms and research labs.

One important tool for analyzing particles is a stereobinocular microscope, also called a stereoscopic microscope. It consists of two microscopes mounted side by side with a single eyepiece. The viewer can perceive height differences on an object—in other words, the image is three-dimensional. With these microscopes, light is reflected off the surface of an object rather than shined through it. This type of microscope is useful in examining larger objects and solid objects.

A comparison microscope also uses two compound microscopes with one combined viewing unit. Unlike the stereoscopic microscope, however, in which both microscopes are focused on the same point, the two microscopes in a comparison microscope are focused on different points. This way, the viewer can view two objects at the same time. It's also possible to see one object superimposed over another. The comparison microscope is used for side-by-side comparison of particles such as hairs and fibers.

A polarizing microscope has a light source equipped with a polarizing filter, or polarizer, so that the light is *polarized*—the light waves vibrate in a specific direction rather than randomly in all directions as in ordinary light. A polarizing microscope is used to examine minerals and crystals, because these objects change light as it passes through them. Under the polarizing microscope, these changes are seen as color changes.

If objects are too small to be examined with an ordinary microscope, then scientists use an electron microscope. This instrument uses a flow of electrons rather than light rays to produce an image that is magnified up to one million times.

THE SE

Selma Paint and Supply Company occupies two small offices on the second floor of an old wooden building that, ironically, is in need of paint. Detectives Sullivan and Vasquez climb the rickety stairs. At the end of a narrow hallway is a glass door. They knock.

"Come in, the door's open," a voice calls.

Two men are seated at separate desks, surrounded by piles of papers and several telephones. Neither man gets up, but the older one says, "What can we do for you?"

Sullivan speaks as she shows her badge. "We're Detectives Sullivan and Vasquez. Fairfax County Police."

The older man gets up from his chair at once. He pushes his hand nervously through his white hair. "Listen, officer, I know I haven't filed my gross receipts tax return, but we've been. . . ."

Sullivan holds up her hand. "No. This isn't about taxes. We're investigating a murder."

"A murder?!"

"Is Ann Marlboro an employee here?"

"Yeah, she's our bookkeeper. Works part-time, two days a week. Why?"

"She's been murdered."

"Oh, my God." The old man sits back down. "How? Why? Who would want to kill her?"

"That's what we're investigating." Sullivan moves some files from a chair. "Mind if we sit down?"

"Oh, no. Not at all."

Vasquez empties a second chair and sits down.

"When was the last time you saw Ann Marlboro?" Sullivan asks.

"It's been over a week. She didn't come in this week. When I called, I got her message machine. I think she said something about going to Ohio to visit her in-laws. But I'm not sure."

Then Vasquez speaks. "If this is a paint and supply company, where's your paint and supplies?" He waves his arms around the room, which contains the desks, numerous file cabinets, computers, and an old fax machine. Papers and files are stacked everywhere.

"We don't do retail," explains the older man. "We buy paint and paint supplies from manufacturers and jobbers and resell them to large users—mostly county and state governments. No cans of paint here. We never see the paint."

The younger man pulls open a file drawer and hands the detectives a brochure listing the company's products and prices. Vasquez studies the paper, then says, "How many manufacturers and jobbers do you buy from?"

"Oh, fifteen. Maybe twenty."

"Do you have a list of your suppliers?"

"I can print one out for you." A few moments later, he hands the list to Sullivan.

"Do you ever visit these places?" asks Sullivan, looking at the printout.

"Sometimes, but not often."

"One more thing," says Sullivan. "Can I see one of your blank invoice forms?"

The younger man hands her a form. It has a white original backed by pink, yellow, and green copies.

"Who has access to these?" Vasquez asks.

"We both do. Ann did, too. She kept our books and did our filing, including invoicing." The two men look at each other, clearly puzzled. "What does that have to do with her murder?"

Sullivan leans forward in her chair. "I'm not sure," she says. "We just need background. Have you had any money missing?"

"No." The younger man speaks emphatically. "Ann handled our bank stuff, but we have an accountant check everything once a month and nothing's been wrong."

"Do you have a copy of invoice A16482?"

"Why, sure." The man opens and closes several file drawers, thumbs through files, and finally produces a folder. "It should be in here." Then he pauses, goes back to the cabinet, and removes more folders. Shaking his head, he says, "I don't know where you got that number, but we don't have a number like that."

"Do you have an A1648?" Sullivan asks.

"Yeah, that's more like it." He opens a folder. "What do you know. Our invoices come in books of twenty-five, and A1626 through A1650 are missing." He thumbs through the folder. "We have A1601 to A1625, then a sheet of paper that says 'Packet missing, pick up at A1651.'" He scratches his head. "That's odd. But all the records and receipts are in order. These invoices are from last year."

"What do you make of this?" Sullivan passes a copy of the invoice found at the murder scene to the younger man. "Is this one of your customers in Ruckersville?"

Both men look at the invoice. "This is our invoice, but it's not our invoice number and we have no customer by that name," says the older man. "Besides, why would a hardware store order only ten gallons of paint? The usual orders are for much more."

"Any ideas?" asks Sullivan.

"Not a clue."

"If you don't mind, we'd like to hold on to this file," says Sullivan, carefully placing it into her briefcase.

"Sure. Do you think Ann took those blank invoices? And if she did, do they have something to do with her murder?" asks the younger man.

"We don't have answers, only questions," Sullivan responds. "We may have more questions later—so don't leave town."

Back in the car, Sullivan says, "We've got their prints on these papers just in case they match the ones at the crime scene, but I don't think they're likely suspects."

While Vasquez drives, Sullivan calls in to the lab. "Any luck with the stuff from the carpet?"

"Plenty."

"Tell me."

"First, the microscopic analysis of the fibers showed that they were cotton and were dyed blue. Infrared spectroscopy, gas chromatography, and mass spectroscopy told us that the dye was aniline type and azure blue. The dye was a permanent dye. So we conclude that the fibers were from denim jeans or denim work clothes. Other fibers were consistent with the subject's clothing and the carpeting in the bedroom."

"Anything else?"

"The particle analysis was interesting. We found traces of dust that contain quartz, red clay, and . . ."

" . . . and?"

" . . . and calcite and oil."

"Anything else?"

"Not yet. I need to talk to Morrie on the minerals and Bill on the oil. I'll get back to you."

Sullivan looks at Vasquez. "I have an idea."

Vasquez looks at her expectantly.

"We're near the university. Let's pop in on my friends the professors."

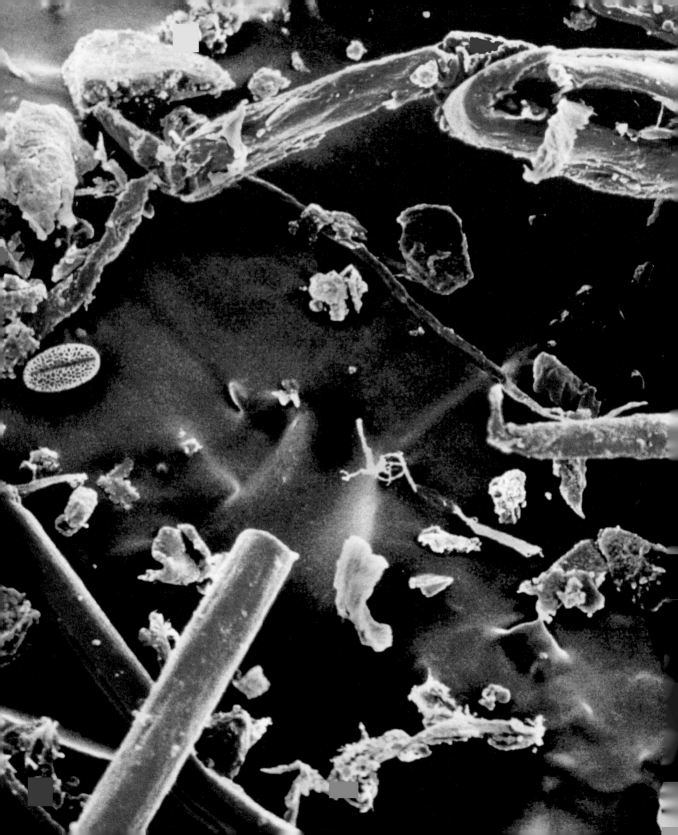

Chapter Five

DIRT TALKS:
FORENSIC GEOCHEMISTRY

The two detectives sit uncomfortably in folding chairs in the office of the chairman of the chemistry department at George Mason University, in the heart of the old city of Fairfax.

Professor George Rushmore offers them coffee. "My colleague, Doug Mose, is the geologist you need. He should be here soon."

"We appreciate your time," says Sullivan.

Rushmore is short, with thinning hair and a pleasant smile. He wears the expected tweed jacket. "Let me get this straight. You're investigating a murder and you've found traces of calcite and oil at the crime scene and lead in the skin under the victim's fingernails."

"Right."

"And your question for me is?"

"Can you help us identify the source of these items?"

"I can help you with the oil. We can talk about the lead, too, but you'll have to ask Doug about the calcite."

Just then, the door opens. "What's going on?" asks Professor Mose. He is taller than Rushmore and wears colorful suspenders, a full beard, and a wide smile.

A color-enhanced image from an electron microscope showing dust, pollen, and soot particles

Rushmore explains: "These detectives are working on a murder case. They need some scientific advice."

"Have they talked to any scientists?"

Rushmore laughs. "That's us, Doug."

Dr. Mose smiles. "In that case, what can we do for the law?"

When Sullivan finishes explaining their discoveries, Mose nods. "Sounds interesting," he says.

"Let me tell you about lead," Rushmore begins. "Lead occurs naturally in the earth. It is mined and then refined to its pure state. After that, it's combined with other chemicals for many purposes. Lead carbonate, for example, is the pigment that was once commonly used in white paint. It has very desirable paint characteristics—it holds color and makes paint flow easily from brush to surface. But it's poison! Lead poisoning can cause brain and nervous system disorders and can lead to death. Many children have been poisoned by chewing on surfaces painted with lead-based paint. When lead-free latex paints became popular in the 1950s and 1960s, the use of lead paint decreased. And in 1978, lead-based paints were banned from residential use."

"And how does that relate here?"

"The lead you have found is lead chromate—from a lead-based paint that is bright yellow. It was once used on road striping and on the outside of school buses." Rushmore studies the two detectives. "I don't know whether any of this helps you or not."

"Well, somehow paint seems to be playing a major role in this mystery," says Vasquez.

Rushmore frowns. "If you have paint samples from different places, your lab should be able to determine if they're the same paint or not. Now, let me tell you about the oil. Most motor oil contains several hundred compounds. We can identify the type of fuel—motor oil, transmission fluid, and so forth. If you provide us with two different samples of oil, we can tell you whether or not they came from the same automobile because trace materials from that automobile will be present in the oil."

FROM ROCKS TO TOXINS

Forensic geologists analyze deposits of crystals, rocks, and soil found at a crime scene or on a suspect or victim. Forensic chemists analyze bomb fragments, residue from fires, and other chemicals related to crimes. Chemistry is also involved in the investigation of food tampering, pollution, and dangerous working conditions.

A special type of forensic chemist is the toxicologist, a scientist who investigates toxins, or poisons. Forensic toxicologists look for illegal drugs in suspects. This can be done with hair samples, breath samples, blood samples, or urine samples. A toxicologist may also investigate a death caused by drugs, carbon monoxide or other gases, or poisons.

At an autopsy, a medical examiner collects tissue and organ samples that the toxicologist will examine. The location of the chemicals in the body and organs can provide information about how the chemical got into the victim. Was it swallowed, injected, or inhaled? The toxicologist may also be able to determine when the chemical entered the body.

CHROMATOGRAPHY AND SPECTROSCOPY

Chromatographic and spectroscopic instruments are used to identify the chemical makeup of a wide variety of materials, from drugs and poisons to the chemicals used in lighting fires. The chromatography process separates materials into their basic

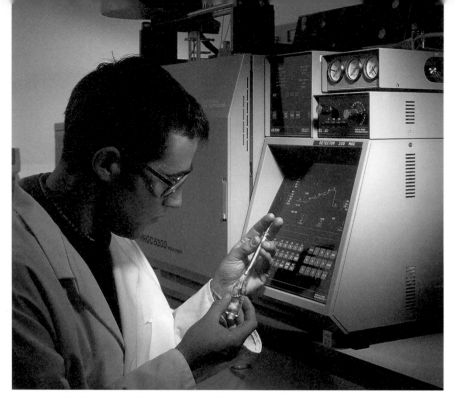

A toxicologist uses chromatography to analyze toxic substances such as poisons and drugs.

molecular components. For example, ink can be broken down into its individual dyes, and solvents can be analyzed.

One instrument used to separate materials is called a gas chromatograph. The material to be analyzed is forced through tubes packed with tiny beads. Large molecules will pass around the beads, while smaller molecules are absorbed through pores in the beads. As a result, smaller molecules pass through the tubes more slowly, and all the molecules are separated by size. This technique is extremely accurate and can detect minute amounts (one part per million parts) of toxic substances, pesticides, or drugs.

The gas chromatograph works in tandem with another specialized instrument called a mass spectrometer. This device analyzes the basic components of a sample material. It uses light to identify various molecules and produces a "readout," or visual image of the molecules. This image, called a spectrogram, can be matched with spectrograms made from known chemicals. The spectrometer works because different molecules absorb light at different wavelengths. Each molecule presents a unique, identifiable spectrogram.

There are many other forms of spectroscopy, such as fluorescence spectroscopy, infrared spectroscopy, atomic adsorption spectroscopy, and X-ray spectroscopy. These techniques can be used alone or together to analyze any substance.

One area of forensic science where these techniques are used extensively is forensic toxicology. Fluid samples such as blood, stomach juices, saliva, and urine obtained during an autopsy are often sent to forensic toxicology labs, as are samples of organs and other body tissues. Toxicologists use chromatography and spectroscopy to find and identify any drugs or poisons in the samples.

THE CASE

Sullivan glances at her watch, then asks, "Now, Dr. Mose, what can you tell us about calcite?"

"Calcite, hmm. Calcite is calcium carbonate—limestone. In finely powdered form, it is the basic ingredient of concrete and cement. Calcite is found in nature in many places.

"Here in Virginia, limestone is found throughout the Shenandoah Valley and in a different form in the caverns on the western side of the Blue Ridge Mountains. When groundwater seeps into holes and cracks in the limestone terrain, calcite in the stone dissolves and trickles downward into the caverns. There, the water drips ever so slowly, depositing the calcite into those formations you see in the caves—stalagmites and stalactites. They look something like icicles. The calcite deposits in the dripping water form stalactites, which hang down from the top of the cave. Then, when the water drops to the floor, the calcite builds up from below as stalagmites."

Water dripping through soil containing calcite builds stalactites on the top (remember the "c" as in "ceiling") and stalagmites on the bottom (remember the "g" as in "ground") of many caves.

"Is there any way to tell if our calcite is from concrete or a cave or just anywhere?" Vasquez asks.

"We'd need to look at the particles under a microscope."

"Our lab did that," says Sullivan, already dialing to request a fax.

When copies of the microscope prints arrive over the fax machine, Professor Mose studies them. "Yes. We have something here. These particles of calcite have been crystallized. What this tells us is that the calcite sample you have came from a cavern."

"Like the Endless Cavern or Luray Caverns?"

"Yes, or any of several others. There are a lot of caves along the western slopes of the Blue Ridge Mountains. Here, I'll show you." Mose leaves the room and returns a few moments later with a map. Stretching it out on a table, he points to an area alongside the mountains. "There are a number of caverns along here. Great tourist attractions."

"My hunch is that this sample came from someplace not too far away," Sullivan says. "Could you identify the cavern by the calcite?"

Mose pulls on his beard. "Well, yes. If you bring me a calcite sample from a specific cave, I can tell you whether that cave was the source of the calcite found under the fingernails of that unfortunate lady."

"It's a good start," says Sullivan. "Now the calcite is talking to us."

Mose laughs. "George, I think these people are weirder than we are!"

"Probably," says Sullivan. "Thank you, gentlemen."

Later, when Sullivan calls Dr. Rushmore, he tells her that the oil found under Ann Marlboro's fingernails is motor oil from a very dirty truck engine. After they hang up, she calls the sheriff of Shenandoah County, who agrees to send two deputies to every known cavern along the western slopes of the Blue Ridge Mountains. They will collect samples of stalagmites from each cavern.

Chapter Six

SKULL AND BONES:
FORENSIC ANTHROPOLOGY

The county sheriff is a tall, large-boned man with a thick shock of graying hair. He drives Sullivan and Vasquez in his old Land Rover to the entrance of Laurel's Cavern, at the base of the Blue Ridge Mountains. They travel on gullied, twisting roads through a stand of pine trees. The sheriff explains that Laurel's Cavern is not a tourist attraction like the Luray Caverns a few miles to the north. This cave does not attract much interest because it is narrow, has low ceilings, and does not cut very deep under the mountain.

"I still don't see why you wanted to come all the way out here to look in this cavern," says the sheriff. "I would've looked for you if I knew what y'all were huntin' for."

"We'd have asked if we knew," says Sullivan.

Both detectives are wearing blue jeans, waterproof boots, heavy jackets, and wool knit caps. They know it will be cold and damp in the cave. "All we know is calcite."

"Calcite?"

"Calcite is the material that stalactites and stalagmites are made of—the formations in the caves that look like icicles," Vasquez explains.

Facial reconstruction, a fascinating branch of forensic anthropology, mixes art with science to create a likeness from a victim's skull.

"OK. But why are we here?" The sheriff scratches his head.

"Because at the murder scene, someone left traces—microscopic traces—of calcite in the carpet," Sullivan says.

"And?"

"Remember that we had your two deputies collect calcite samples from all the caverns on this side of the mountains?"

"Yep."

"Well, our lab people examined the samples, and the one from this cavern matched the tiny particles of calcite we found at the crime scene."

"So what do you think is here?" asks the sheriff.

"That's the trouble," says Sullivan. "We don't have any idea. We're trying to figure out what the murderer or the victim, or someone else who was in that bedroom, was doing in this cavern."

The sheriff shakes his head and points to the narrow opening of the cavern. "It's a small cave with low ceilings," he says, eyeing Sullivan and Vasquez. "It's not going to be easy. You'd better be luckier than you are smart."

The three put on miner's hats, which have lights on the front to illuminate the way. In addition, they each carry a lantern. One by one, they slide down into the dark entrance of the cave. Crouching low, they make their way slowly, following what appears to be the only route. Sullivan leads the way and the sheriff brings up the rear. Sullivan and Vasquez do not notice that the sheriff unwinds a ball of twine behind him to ensure that they can retrace their route.

After an hour of stooping and crawling, they reach an area that seems to be the end of the cavern. A small pool of dark water is on one side, and they hear the sound of dripping water. Their voices echo when they speak.

"Mind if I rest a moment?" asks Vasquez, breathing heavily and sweating, even in the chill of the damp cave.

"We all need a rest," says the sheriff.

As the three settle on the floor of the cavern, the lights from their hats create strange patterns among the craggy stalactites and stalagmites. Sullivan sweeps her lantern in a circle around her as she explores the room. Suddenly, she stops. "Look!"

She shines her light on a place where all the stalagmites are missing.

Cautiously the sheriff edges to the end of the light. "Well, I'll be danged." He runs his hand over the floor of the cave. "They're broken off. All of them." He holds up his lantern to illuminate the area. Then he points down.

Sullivan and Vasquez join him. He is pointing at a human skull and a single bone.

FORENSIC ANTHROPOLOGY

Anthropology is the study of human beings—their physical characteristics, environment, and culture. Forensic anthropology applies the tools of this study to the task of identifying skeletal remains—bones. A forensic anthropologist tries to establish who the bones belonged to and, if possible, the cause of death.

The first step is to determine if the bones are human or animal. A human skull has a distinctive shape and is easily recognized. If the skull is broken or missing, teeth are the next best indicator, since human teeth are unique. They can be identified by their shape and chewing features. Plant-eating animals usually have rows of grinding teeth. Meat eaters have sharply pointed teeth for stabbing and killing and tearing through meat. Human teeth are somewhere between the two. The back teeth are suited for grinding, while the sharper front teeth are good for chopping and slicing. Other bones that are distinctive in humans are the pelvic girdle and the scapula, or shoulder blade.

After establishing that the remains are human, the anthropologist then tries to determine the age, sex, race, and size of the deceased person. If a complete skeleton is recovered, the anthropologist's job is easier. With an intact skeleton, it's possible to tell the person's sex, the age within a five-year range, the approximate size, and often, the race.

To determine sex, forensic anthropologists study the structure and form of the pelvic bones. In females, the hips are wider and the pelvic bone is more angular and open to allow for childbearing. Male hips are narrower. The bony area just below the bottom of the backbone—the sacrum—is wider and larger in males.

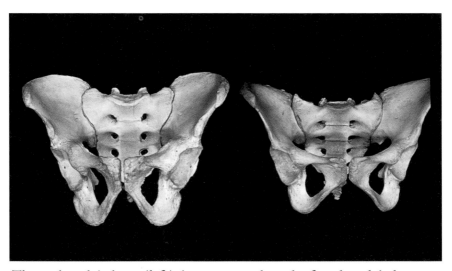

The male pelvic bone (left) *is narrower than the female pelvic bone* (right) *but has a wider and larger sacral area below the backbone.*

The skull can also indicate the sex of the deceased. In males, the browridge—the bone above the eyes covered by the eyebrows—generally juts out more.

To determine age, the anthropologist usually looks first at the teeth, particularly in children. During the period when a child is making the transition from baby teeth to permanent teeth, it's easy to determine age.

Sometimes teeth can be thinly sliced in cross section to determine age. Using an electron microscope, the scientist looks at the layers of material covering the main tissue of the tooth. As a person grows, more layers develop.

The bone joints are also examined. Growth at each bony joint varies at different ages. Examinations of joints and teeth allow the forensic anthropologist to estimate age up to twenty-five years.

Beyond maturity, estimates of age are more difficult. Just as it can be hard to tell a person's age by sight when they are alive, it is difficult to determine their age by their bare bones. A valuable bone for determining age is the clavicle, or collarbone. Age can also be determined by taking X rays of the long bones of the legs. The X rays may reveal the natural thinning of bone (decreased bone density) that occurs with advancing age.

Since the 1980s, forensic anthropologists Mehmet Yasar Iscan and Susan R. Loth have developed a standard for determining age by measuring the bone connections from the ribs to the breastbone. They chart nine stages of bone development from age eighteen to seventy.

In identifying a person's race from skeletal remains, anthropologists recognize three major racial groups: Caucasoid, Mongoloid, and Negroid. These classifications are not based on skin color but on features of the skull and other skeletal traits. For

Forensic Odontology

A forensic odontologist, or dentist, studies teeth and teeth marks to identify a victim or suspect in a crime. Using equipment such as X rays, infrared and ultraviolet photography, electron microscopy, and computer analysis, the forensic odontologist compares teeth or tooth fragments with bite marks or dental records. This specially trained dentist looks at the size and shape of the tooth and its roots; crooked, jagged, or missing teeth; ridges, fillings, chips, and grooves; and spaces between teeth. Also examined are the angle and size of tooth sockets in a jawbone or part of a jaw. Even if teeth are badly damaged, they can often be used as a means of identification.

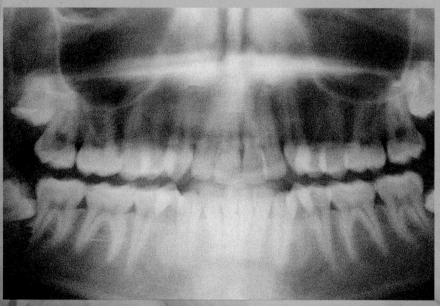

X rays of teeth can often identify a victim. This person's lower wisdom teeth are impacted (wedged between the jawbone and another tooth).

example, in Caucasoids, the femur (the thigh bone) is curved, while in Negroids the femur is straight.

To estimate the person's size, the most important bones are the major leg bones, the femur and the tibia. By measuring the femur and the tibia, the anthropologist can calculate the size of the deceased person. The victim's weight may also be revealed in the wear on the bones at certain points.

Finally, an examination of prominent crests and ridges on the bones, as well as their roughness, shows how muscular the person was. The crests and ridges are places where muscle was attached. A person with little muscle will have smooth bony surfaces. This characteristic applies to both men and women. By looking at muscle development in the arms, the anthropologist can tell whether the person was right-handed or left-handed.

Forensic anthropologists also look for specific characteristics that can identify the victim. Many diseases and injuries leave evidence in the bones. For example, if a person suffered an accident or injury resulting in a broken bone, the bone will show callus formation where it was fractured. Often, X rays on file with a doctor or hospital can be compared to the bone. The best identifier is dental work, which can be compared to the victim's dental records to make a quick match.

A person's occupation can often be deduced from his or her bones. Certain characteristics are so common that they have nicknames, such as milker's neck, cowboy thumb, seamstress's fingers, miner's knee, and weaver's bottom. A vigorous tennis player will show more bone wear and larger muscle development on one arm than the other.

One of the most fascinating areas of forensic anthropology involves facial reconstruction. This is a marriage of art and science. It involves sketching a picture or creating a sculpture of the deceased person's head and face, based on the skull alone. Various characteristics of skulls give a good indication of what the facial features were. For example, the shape of the jawbone predicts whether the lower lip stuck out or not. Still, many details are left to the artist, who cannot tell from the bones whether the person was fat or thin, the hair color and style, and the eye color.

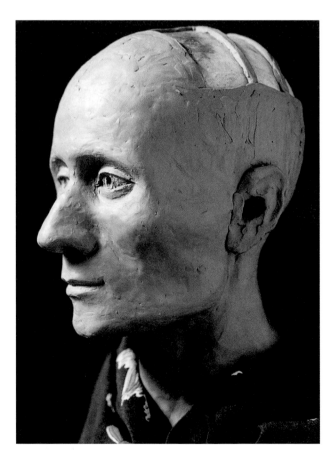

Forensic anthropologists use the shape of a skull to create a model of a dead person's head and face.

THE CASE

Sullivan sits on the edge of her desk and looks at her partner, who is sitting behind the desk across from her. "What do you make of this?" She points to the forensic anthropologist's report.

The skull, the report says, belonged to an Asian male, approximately thirty-five years old with a medium build. Oddly, the bones show traces of mild, barely detectable lead poisoning.

"Paint," says Vasquez.

"Paint?"

"Yes. Remember, some older paints contain lead. So he was involved with paint."

"But how?" Sullivan shakes her head. "We need to visit the paint supply houses on that list we have from Selma Paint." She stands up and thumps her fist into her palm. "And we need to look at their payroll records for the last several years. Maybe there will be an Asian employee who suddenly disappeared from the payroll." She pauses. "I think that skull was talking to us."

"Spooky."

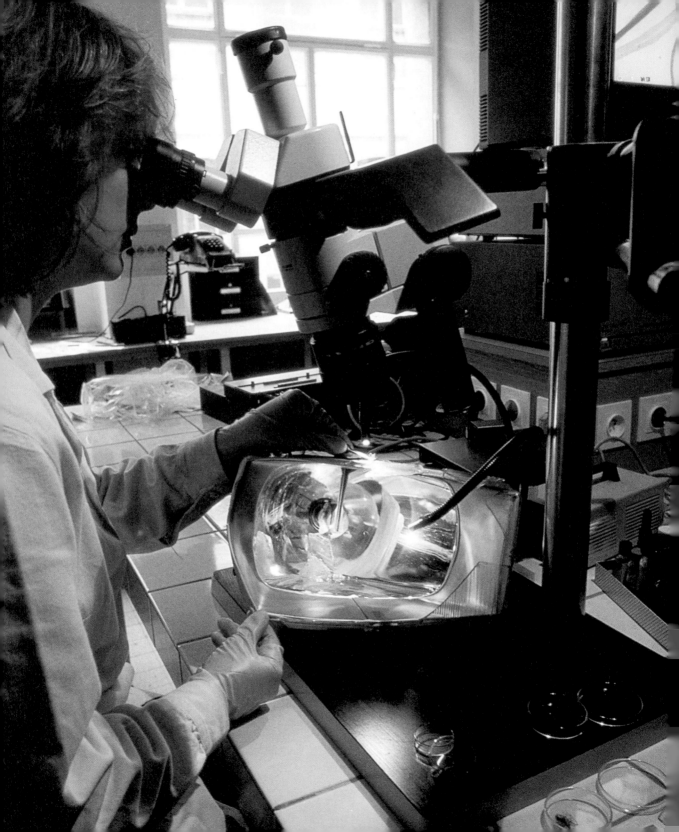

Chapter Seven

ASSEMBLING THE FACTS:
PROBABLE CAUSE

THE CASE

It is late afternoon by the time Detectives Sullivan and Vasquez arrive at the third paint supply house on their list. No evidence turned up at the first two warehouses.

This place looks different. It is run-down and abandoned. There is no sign of activity—no cars, no people, no lights.

The two officers park by a door in the front, next to a large gravel area. The door's window is dirty, and there is no bell or knocker. Above the door is a rusty sign: "Conroy Delman, Paints."

"Looks abandoned," says Sullivan.

"The building does, but this driveway and parking area have been used," says Vasquez. "No grass is growing in the gravel."

They get out of the car and walk along the side of the building. A battered, dirty 1980 Ford pickup is parked outside. Vasquez notes the license plate number. Getting down on his hands and knees, he scrapes some oil-soaked red clay from under the truck. He puts the sample into a small plastic bag. "Who knows?" he says.

The two detectives continue to walk the length of the building. The doors above the loading dock are locked. "The doors are old and rough, but the chain and lock are new," Vasquez observes.

Even the smallest chip of glass collected from a hit-and-run victim can be matched to a headlight, connecting a specific car to the crime.

"Let's see if we can find anybody inside," says Sullivan.

As they turn, Vasquez stops. "Hey. Look!" He points to two sets of old footprints, barely visible in the dirt. One set of prints is from a woman's shoe.

"This may be a break," says Sullivan. "Remember the brown shoes? If the killer replaced the victim's shoes, maybe it was because there was mud on them and he figured the dirt could be traced. And he was right. What he didn't know was that tiny particles of dirt were left in the carpet where she walked. If those microtraces match the clay here, we've got a connection."

"We'll need a picture of these prints and a sample of the clay," Vasquez says excitedly. He takes a series of pictures while Sullivan gathers several samples of the soil near the prints.

"Got it," Sullivan says. "Now let's see if anybody's home."

They walk to the front of the building. Vasquez bangs on the door. There is no answer. He tries the knob. The door creaks open. Inside, sunlight illuminates a musty office. "Hello!" Vasquez shouts. He and Sullivan do not enter the room but instead stand at the threshold.

A door opens in the back of the office. A heavyset man with a dark beard and long scraggly hair peers out. His face is smudged with dirt and there's paint on his overalls.

"What do you want?" His voice is gruff.

Sullivan flashes her badge. "We're detectives from the Fairfax County Police Department. We'd like to talk to you."

"I got nothing to say to police."

"May we come in?"

"Got nothin' to say."

"Is there something you don't want us to know?" Sullivan asks.

"You got no business here. If you want to arrest me, tell me what for; if not, go away."

"Can we look around for a minute?"

"Not unless you got a search warrant!" He slams the rear office door shut and disappears into the warehouse.

"We'll be back," says Sullivan quietly as she and Vasquez retreat to their car.

From the car, Sullivan calls the permits division of the Fairfax County Department of Environment Services. She learns that the occupancy permit for the warehouse is issued to someone named Lo Ming Chow, who lives in the nearby area known as Shirlington.

The detectives hurry to Chow's address, which turns out to be a crowded rooming house. They ask the landlord about Chow. The landlord shrugs his shoulders and says that he hardly knew the Chinese man and hasn't seen him in over a year. "He went off without paying his last month's rent," he says. "All he left was a few clothes."

Looking at each other, the two detectives say at the same time, "Warehouse." They hurry to police headquarters to begin the process of writing an affidavit—the sworn statement they must prepare to apply for a search warrant. Only with a search warrant will they have the right to enter the warehouse without permission from the occupant.

SEARCH WARRANTS

In many countries, police have the authority to enter people's homes or businesses at any time to search for evidence of a crime. This is not true in the United States. Police cannot enter a home or business without a search warrant. A search warrant is an official paper issued by a judge or magistrate authorizing the police or other law enforcement officers to enter a specified place and conduct a search as defined in the warrant.

A search without a warrant is illegal. If evidence of a crime is found during an unauthorized search, then that evidence cannot be used in court at the criminal trial. Such evidence is considered tainted, or "fruit of the poisoned tree," a phrase first used by Supreme Court Justice William Brennan. Often criminals are found not guilty at a trial because the evidence against them was discovered during an unauthorized search.

The use of the search warrant in the United States stems from the Bill of Rights, the first ten amendments to the Constitution. The Fourth Amendment states: "The right of the people to be secure in their persons, houses, papers, and effects, against unreasonable searches and seizure, shall not be violated, and no Warrants shall issue, but upon probable cause, supported by Oath of affirmation, and particularly describing the place to be searched, and the persons or things to be seized." Over the years, the amendment has been interpreted and upheld by the U.S. Supreme Court, providing law enforcement officials with guidelines to follow in conducting searches.

To conduct a search, law enforcement officers must first go to a judicial officer. Under oath, the officers present evidence suggesting there is "probable cause" to believe that they will find more significant evidence of criminal activity in the location they wish to search.

Probable cause lies somewhere between "I know a crime is being committed" and "I think one is." Suspicion or belief is not enough. Each case rests on the specific facts. The judge or magistrate issuing the warrant must weigh the facts and decide whether there is probable cause to believe that evidence will be found at a particular place or on a particular person.

The standard declared by the Supreme Court is called the "totality of the circumstances" test. In each case, the judge

Police investigators must obtain a search warrant from a judicial officer before they can look for evidence on private property.

must look at all the facts and circumstances presented by the police. For example, Detective Sullivan's sworn statement seeking a warrant to search the paint warehouse would present the following evidence:

1) footprints found at the paint warehouse matched the shoe size of the victim;

2) clay from outside the paint warehouse matched clay particles found at the crime scene;

3) a forged paint invoice was recovered at the crime scene.

The judge will likely conclude that this is enough evidence to suggest that evidence of a crime will likely be found in the warehouse. A search warrant will be issued.

Search warrants are not general. They state the exact place to be searched, what is being sought (such as paint), and what persons or items are to be seized.

Minute particles of soil, tar, fibers, and even residues of fluids found on the sole of a shoe can be important circumstantial evidence.

Courts recognize two types of evidence, direct and circumstantial. If a witness testifies about something of which he or she has personal knowledge, that is direct evidence. If a witness testifies that he saw a suspect shoot a victim, that is direct evidence. A videotape or photograph of a suspect robbing a store is also direct evidence. On the other hand, circumstantial evidence is based on inference, when facts can be reasonably determined or connected according to common experience. If a gun is found with a suspect's fingerprints on it, and the bullet that killed the victim matches the gun, this circumstantial evidence suggests that the suspect used the gun to kill the suspect.

THE  CASE

"OK, here's what we've got," says Sullivan as Vasquez inches the car along in the rush-hour traffic. Sullivan lists the circumstantial evidence they will present when they apply for a search warrant.

"A thirty-two-year-old bookkeeper for Selma Paint and Supply Company has been murdered. The company is not missing any money, but a package of invoices is missing. One copy showed up at the murder scene. The serial number of this invoice was altered."

"And," says Vasquez, "a shoe print found outside one of Selma's suppliers, a paint warehouse, matches the subject's shoes. Soil samples from outside the warehouse also match microscopic traces at the murder scene."

"Lead from lead-based paint was found under the fingernails of the victim," says Sullivan.

"Yes, and calcite found at the murder scene matches calcite from the cavern where a skull and bone were found."

Sullivan continues, "A forensic anthropologist has tentatively identified the skull as belonging to an Asian male, and the paint warehouse belongs to a Chinese man named Lo Ming Chow."

"According to Chow's landlord, Chow hasn't been around for over a year," adds Vasquez.

"Yes," says Sullivan. "I think we have enough for probable cause."

After reading the detectives' sworn statement, the magistrate agrees and issues a search warrant. Armed with the warrant, Sullivan and Vasquez, along with four backup police squads, roar into the parking area of the warehouse.

Chapter Eight

SOUND EVIDENCE:
AUDIO RECONSTRUCTION

THE

Police cars are spread out across the parking area as Sullivan, leading the group of officers, approaches the front door of the paint warehouse. The front door is hanging wide open. The officers quickly enter the office and find that it has been ransacked. Papers are scattered across the floor. File drawers are open and emptied.

They push open the rear door of the office and shout, "Police! We're here to execute a search. Anyone here should come out."

There is no reply.

"Didn't wait for us," says Vasquez, waving his hand at the trashed office. "I think our surly friend was in a hurry to leave."

Passing through the rear office door, they step into the vast space of the warehouse. It Is filled with lumber, old hardware, and bags of fertilizer, sand, and garden mulch. Some of the bags have been ripped open.

"What are we looking for?" asks one of the police officers.

"The first thing would be paint," says Vasquez.

"And a telephone with an answering machine," adds Sullivan.

*Waveform analysis uses visual representation of sound waves to
identify voice characteristics.*

Slowly the team moves through the piles of materials and supplies strewn around the concrete floor.

"Here's some paint," calls an officer from the far corner of the room. Sullivan and Vasquez hurry over.

Under a large canvas tarp are more than one hundred cans of paint. The brands and colors are all mixed up.

"What a mess! How can they know their inventory?" Vasquez says.

"I don't think paint is the real product here," says Sullivan. "Some of these cans are old. Some have been opened and closed."

She removes her Swiss army knife from her pocket and, using the screwdriver, opens a can with paint edging around the top seal.

"Ho!" exclaims Vasquez.

Sullivan lifts a small plastic bag, dripping with bright yellow paint, out of the can. She opens the bag carefully and looks at the pure white powder inside. "Cocaine."

She turns to one of the uniformed officers. "Seal off this building and get forensics and several trucks over here. I want the paint cans, doorknobs, desks, everything, dusted for prints."

"We're on it, Detective Sullivan," says an officer.

She and Vasquez walk quickly back toward the office. Vasquez looks under an overturned chair. "Here's the telephone and answering machine," he says. "And it's not broken." He pushes rewind and listens for messages. There are none. "He's wiped it clean."

"So he thinks," says Sullivan. "I want to take it to the lab. With modern techniques, we can make this machine talk."

AUDIO ANALYSIS

Forensic audio specialists analyze audio recordings to help solve crimes. A recording such as an audiotape can be subjected to a series of analyses. Different techniques yield different types of information, such as how the tape was recorded. When a magnetic tape from a telephone answering machine is erased, it is simply demagnetized. This means that the patterns of magnetic particles that make up the recording become scrambled. The scrambling allows new recordings to be made. Often, the demagnetizing process does not completely remove the recorded sound, so investigators try to remove unwanted sounds and increase the audio quality of the voice on the tape.

Two ways to restore words that have been "erased" are aural analysis and waveform analysis. Aural analysis simply means analyzing spoken words. Waveform analysis uses a visual presentation of the sound waves themselves.

Instruments known as analog equalizers are used to either boost or reduce sound frequencies. Sound, like light, travels in a wave motion, and the waves of many sounds occur in regular, repeated patterns. The number of waves that pass a fixed point per second is referred to as sound frequency, or pitch. The simplest sound wave is a pure tone. Notes played on a musical instrument have more complex waves. A sound wave can become so complex that no particular pitch can be discerned, as in white noise.

In the world of audio recording, sound frequencies, or ranges of sound, are broken into segments, such as bass, midrange, and treble. Bass sounds are deep or low-pitched, while treble sounds are higher in pitch. You may be familiar with these terms from your compact disc or tape player—you can increase or decrease the bass or treble to get better sound. Refined audio instruments can break these ranges into even smaller ranges.

Once a recording is separated into its frequencies, different ranges of sound can be made louder or softer to improve the sound quality. In this way, the frequencies of a voice can be isolated and enhanced. The analog equalizer removes unwanted noises or sound frequencies without affecting the sound of the voice.

Another technique used to clean up noisy audio recordings is called Fast Fourier Transform Digital Noise Reduction, or FFT/DNR. In this process, tapes are digitized (transferred to a computer disk or hard drive), and software algorithms are used to filter out unwanted sounds. Another sophisticated computer analysis, Digital Signal Processing (DSP), also helps audio analysts understand recordings.

Even with the variety of systems and filters available to remove background noise and enhance voice messages, it may still be impossible to recover voice messages from an erased tape. It's usually easier to recover an erased message from an older answering machine than from a newer one.

THE CASE

After Sullivan calls the audio lab to let them know a tape is on its way, she turns to her partner. "OK, let's check the rest room."

"Rest room?"

"Yes. We need hair samples. I want to see if any DNA in this building matches the DNA from under Marlboro's fingernails. The autopsy report indicated that skin debris was recovered. If she scratched the murderer, DNA from the skin might match whatever we find here."

It takes only a minute at the sink to find a few strands of dark hair. Vasquez carefully places each hair in a plastic bag, noting the date and place of recovery.

Sophisticated computer programs are used to remove unwanted noises and to enhance voices from audio recordings.

"Now," Sullivan says, "let's see what those officers have found in the warehouse." As they enter the warehouse, one of the police officers calls out: "Over here! Here's two more."

The officer brings the paint cans to the detectives. Sullivan opens one of them and removes a second bag of cocaine. The bag is dripping with paint, but the white powder inside is dry and protected.

Meanwhile, Vasquez opens the second can. "Ho!"

"What?"

With a paint-covered rubber glove on his hand, he lifts out a pistol.

"The objects in this place are not just talking to us, they're screaming," says Sullivan. Wrapping the paint-soaked gun in plastic, she hands it to a nearby officer. "Please get this over to the lab right away," she says.

As they wait for the results, Sullivan calls Dr. Rushmore at the university. "What do you make of the oil sample from under the truck?"

"You must have radar," says Rushmore. "I just finished the test. It's a match. The oil under the victim's fingernails, scratched from the skin of her attacker, is a close match to the chemical characteristics of the oil sample you sent me from beneath the truck."

"Great work," says Sullivan.

"And it's an old truck, too," adds Rushmore.

"Thanks." Sullivan turns to Vasquez. "He's our man."

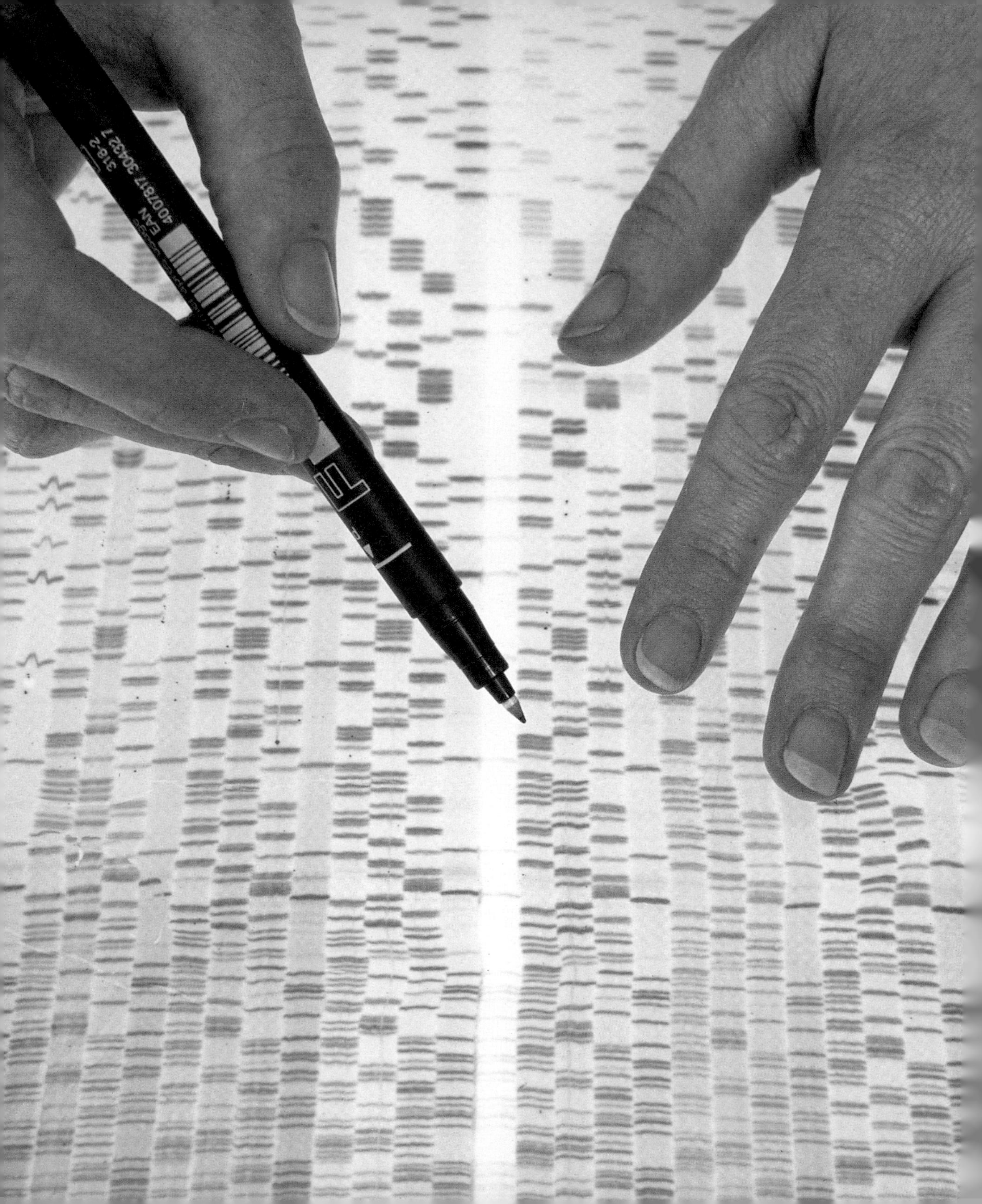
EAN
4007817 304321
318-2

Chapter Nine

UNIQUE TRACES:
FINGERPRINTING AND
DNA TESTING

THE CASE

The next day, Sullivan and Vasquez spend the morning interviewing Timothy Marlboro. He reveals that his wife seemed extremely tense over the past several months, but he never learned why. Marlboro also mentions that he couldn't find his .22 target pistol.

After Marlboro leaves, the report comes back from the fingerprint lab. The house contained only the prints of Timothy, Ann, their son, Tim, and a cleaning lady who came once a week. But there was one strange print on the doorknob. The print could not be identified. Whoever left this print had never been fingerprinted for any reason—the person had never been arrested, was not in the military service, and was not employed by a company that required a security clearance.

FINGERPRINTING

If you look closely at the tips of your fingers, you'll see many tiny ridges that form patterns. When you touch something,

A forensic scientist reads the results of a DNA test on an autoradiograph.

[85]

sweat and body oils on your fingertips leave an impression of those ridges on the surface of the object. This impression is a fingerprint. It is astonishing to realize that of the billions of people on earth, no two people, not even identical twins, have the same fingerprints. For this reason, fingerprint identification can often conclusively tie a suspect to a crime. If the suspect's fingerprints are found on the murder weapon or at the crime scene, and the person had no other reason to be at that location, then the fingerprints are strong evidence of guilt.

When detectives arrive at a crime scene, one of the first things they do is look for fingerprints. Experienced investigators know where to look for prints. They start by checking points of entry and exit in the building. They look at items that have been disturbed, such as a broken lamp or overturned chair, and examine things that a criminal might be likely to touch, including door handles, telephones, and light switches.

Fingerprints at a crime scene may be visible if the suspect's hands were soiled with dirt, grease, or blood. These visible prints can be easily photographed. More often, the prints are not visible to the naked eye. In these cases, investigators use different methods to "develop" the prints. The most common technique is to brush a special powder onto the surface that is thought to bear prints. Investigators use a black powder on light objects and a light gray powder on dark objects. A light brushing brings out the impression of the print. Then the fingerprint is "lifted" by pressing sticky tape onto the powder.

Chemicals can be used to lift fingerprints from absorbent surfaces such as clothing. Lasers (high-energy light sources) also make some prints visible. Moisture and oils reflect laser light as a yellow glow that can be photographed. This technique is often used to recover fingerprints from a victim's skin.

The fingerprints on this glove were revealed by magnetic fingerprint powder. The powder consists of tiny iron flakes that stick to the greasy residue of a print. The excess powder is removed by a magnet.

Law enforcement agencies classify fingerprint patterns into three main types: loops, arches, and whorls. A fourth pattern called "accidental" or "composite" combines parts of all three types but is commonly considered a subtype of the whorl pattern.

Anyone who is arrested is fingerprinted, and the fingerprint is placed on file with the Federal Bureau of Investigation. The agency has more than two hundred million prints on file. These files are computerized, and the FBI's Integrated Automated Fingerprint Identification System electronically compares any fingerprint submitted by law enforcement officers anywhere in the country to prints in the FBI system. The task of fingerprint matching used to be done by hand—the fingerprints were filed on cards—which could take as long as twenty days. This burdensome task has been reduced to a mere two hours and is getting faster all the time.

Fingerprints are only one type of impression that detectives focus on during a criminal investigation. Other impressions include palm prints and footprints, footwear impressions, and automobile tire impressions.

DNA TESTING

Of all the recent developments in crime detection, none is more exciting than DNA testing. This highly specific method of identification is sometimes referred to as "DNA fingerprinting."

To understand how DNA testing works, you have to know what DNA is. The human body is made up of cells. The cells may be hair, skin, bone, brain—you get the idea. The human body is made up of more than one hundred trillion cells. Each cell has a nucleus. Inside each nucleus are chromosomes. A chromosome is a tightly coiled spool of a single molecule called DNA. DNA is short for *deoxyribonucleic acid*. This complex molecule is responsible for passing along an individual's personal traits, such as hair and eye color. Half of an individual's forty-six chromosomes are inherited from each parent.

Think of DNA as a personal book of specifications telling how to "construct" one of us. In this book are thousands and thousands of chapters, and each chapter is filled with thousands of words of instruction. Everyone's book has similar chapters—describing hair, heart, kidneys, eyes, nose, and every other body part. While the subjects of the chapters are similar, the exact words in them may be very much alike or very different. Even chapters that are very much alike are never exactly the same for any two people, except identical twins. The words, or perhaps the spelling of the words, varies. Just as every fingerprint is different, every person's DNA is unique. The only exception is identical twins, who share the same DNA.

The DNA molecule has two strands. It looks like a spiral staircase or a ladder that twists into a spiral, which is why it is often referred to as a double helix. If you were to untwist a single chromosome and stretch it straight out, it would be about 6 feet long. Each strand of a DNA molecule is made up of a long chain of chemical units called nucleotides. Nucleotides have three parts: a phosphate, a sugar, and a base. The sides of the ladder are formed by sugars and phosphates; the rungs are formed by pairs of bases bound together.

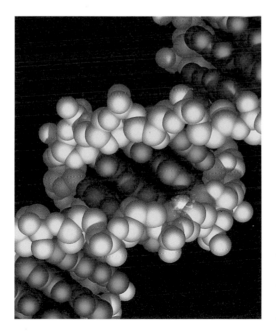

A DNA strand is a single, complex molecule appearing as a spiral ladder of chemical units called nucleotides.

There are four bases. They are the chemicals adenine, cytosine, guanine, and thymine, identified as A, C, G, and T. Each DNA strand is a series, or sequence, of nucleotides containing these bases. Each base binds to a base on the other strand; the bound pair form the rung between the two chains. Adenine always binds to thymine, while cytosine always binds to guanine. Thus, if one strand is A-T-C-G, the other is T-A-G-C. The order of the bases determines their function.

Genes are segments of a DNA molecule. Genes carry the genetic code—a blueprint determining the characteristics that living things pass on to their offspring. Humans are thought to have around thirty thousand genes.

Interestingly, some parts of an individual's "book of specifications" are gibberish. That is, many of the base sequences do not form genes that pass instructions to the cells. The function of these sequences is not completely understood; they probably play a role in regulating the genes. These "nonsense" sequences are called introns. They may occur at any point in a chromosome, even in the middle of a gene.

For a DNA molecule to direct the replication of a cell (to make more skin cells or more liver cells, for example), it must hand off the "blueprint," or instruction book, to another molecule, RNA (ribonucleic acid). RNA assembles individual amino acid molecules—organic compounds composed of carbon, hydrogen, oxygen, nitrogen, and sometimes sulfur—into protein molecules. Protein molecules are complex molecules that are the body's building blocks. As the genetic blueprints from the DNA are copied to the RNA molecules, special restrictive enzymes remove the introns, which are not necessary for cell reproduction. The restrictive enzymes cause a chemical reaction that acts like a molecular scissors, cutting out the intron sequences.

The intron sequences are not needed to make proteins, but they are of great importance to forensic scientists. That's because these sequences form repeating patterns that are unique to every person on earth. This discovery was made in 1984 by Alec Jeffreys, a geneticist at the University of Leicester in England. His finding led to DNA testing.

Jeffreys was using a standard laboratory test for analyzing complex molecules. The test uses a chemical treatment to break molecules into smaller, more easily analyzed pieces. Jeffreys used the test on a DNA sample. An X ray of the resulting solution showed light and dark bands of different widths, like a bar code. Each band represented a segment of DNA. Many other scientists had observed the same series of repeating patterns without realizing the significance of what they were seeing. Jeffreys noticed that the repeating patterns differed significantly for each person. He coined the term "DNA fingerprinting" to describe the process.

Every cell in a person's body contains the same DNA and, therefore, has the same "DNA fingerprint," a fact that led to the development of DNA testing and identification. DNA can be extracted from even the tiniest drop of a body fluid, such as blood or saliva, or from skin, bone, hair, and other body parts. One exception is mature red blood cells. They do not have a nucleus. Thus, they contain no extractable DNA. But red blood cells do contain RNA and enzymes, which also can be used for identification.

HOW DNA TESTING WORKS

DNA testing is a complicated process involving many steps. First, DNA is extracted from a person's blood, sweat, saliva,

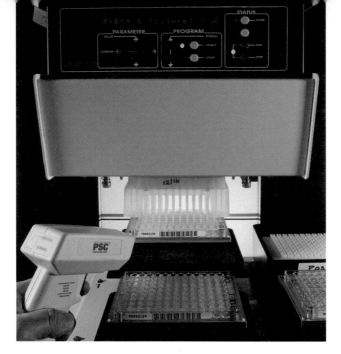

A machine that reads DNA samples with the aid of a computer

hair, or skin. If using blood, the white blood cells are removed and split apart to release the DNA strands. Once a sample is obtained, there are many steps:

• In the laboratory, the DNA is fragmented, using restriction enzymes—the molecular scissors—to cut away fragments of introns. These fragments are replicated into millions and millions of copies. When there is a sufficient mass of fragments, they are placed into solutions that stop the replicating action. Dyes are added to color-code the fragments.

• The solutions containing the fragments are put into a sheet of shallow, gel-filled tubes. An electric charge is sent through the gel, which causes the DNA fragments to be pulled through the gel. The larger molecules move more slowly than the smaller ones. This allows the color-coded molecules to be sorted according to size.

• When the fragments reach the end of the sheet, color-code drops appear and fall out of the tubes. A laser beam reads the colored drops as they appear. The DNA sequences are read by the laser, the way bar code labels are read at a grocery store.

An earlier method of DNA testing used a nylon membrane to blot DNA out of the gel. The result was recorded by placing photographic film against the membrane. This photograph of the test results was called an autoradiograph, or autorad.

The FBI established a DNA database in the fall of 1998. It began with an index of the DNA "gene prints" of 250,000 convicted felons. When three intron fragments (called "base-pair fragments" or "short tandem repeats") from two samples match, there is only one chance in two thousand that they are from different people. If the test reveals nine base-pair matches, the likelihood falls to one chance in one billion. In an abundance of caution, the FBI requires thirteen matches for a positive identification.

DNA Testing in Action

The state of Virginia has been in the forefront in developing DNA databases. It established a statewide database in 1990. Two years later, a woman named Marilyn Bandera was brutally murdered—stabbed 150 times. Since the detectives believed that the killer had left a few drops of his own blood at the scene, blood samples were tested and run through the new database. No matches were found. Then, in early 2000, detectives began routinely resubmitting DNA samples from unsolved cases into the database. This time, a match was found with Mack Reaves III, who had been in jail since 1996 on a robbery charge and was out on probation. Reaves was promptly arrested and charged with the murder.

THE  CASE

As Sullivan and Vasquez are talking, they receive a call from the crime lab. It's the audio technician—he's been able to recover some information from the answering machine tape. "I don't know what it means, but here goes: 'You idiot. They'll be coming back. Get out.' Then there are parts I can't make out, then it picks up with, 'Trash the truck. . . . Carol's on Friday at two.'"

Vasquez looks at Sullivan. "What next?" he asks.

Sullivan snaps her orders. She seems to be thinking and moving at supersonic speed. "All points on that truck. Vasquez, give headquarters the license plate number. We only have two days until Friday. The big question: who is Carol and where is she?" She brushes her hair back from her face. "Is Carol a person or a place?"

"Where do we start?" asks Vasquez.

"In the break room," says Sullivan. "We need some coffee and some fresh ideas."

As they walk down the corridor to the few plastic tables and chairs that serve as a lounge, they are both lost in thought. Sullivan shakes her head as she realizes that she is going to miss her daughter's soccer game. But this search cannot wait. A murderer is out there somewhere.

Vasquez is feeling the excitement of the chase in his first murder case. "Who can Carol be?" he wonders.

In the break room, they each get a cup of coffee and settle at a table. "Now," says Sullivan. "If Carol is a person, the place could be anywhere. If Carol's a place, we probably have a better chance." She pauses. "But where?"

"Wait," says Vasquez. He rushes from the room and returns with a map of Virginia. Spreading it out on the table, he studies the map index. "The invoice is our first clue. The invoice was for a hardware store in Ruckersville, Virginia." He points to a spot on the map. "There. Ruckersville is a small town in the middle of the state."

"Right," says Sullivan. "And the skull was also in Virginia."

Just then, Sullivan's cellular phone rings. She removes it from her pocket. "Sullivan," she says. On the other end, a voice says, "We found the truck. It was abandoned and set on fire near Remington."

"Where's that?"

"In Virginia, near Culpeper."

"OK, thanks." She and Vasquez study the map. "There it is—Culpeper. So, he had to be traveling south on 29." She calls headquarters. "Get me the sheriff's office in Culpeper."

She reaches the sheriff and explains the investigation. "Any place named Carol around there?" she asks.

"Nope," he answers. "Not around these parts. But about fifty miles south of here, in Charlottesville, there's a run-down hangout called Carol's Tea Room. Big joke down there is, 'There ain't no Carol, there ain't no tea, and there ain't no room.' It's a beer joint mostly for college kids and locals."

"Thanks," says Sullivan. Hanging up, she says, "It's worth a shot."

Chapter Ten

CLOSING IN:
BALLISTICS

THE **CASE**

Sullivan knows better, but she's feeling so good about the case that she wants to tease Daniel McCool, the prosecuting attorney for Fairfax County.

"What terrible crime do you want to prosecute today, Sullivan?" asks McCool. "It's already after 5:30. Can't you come in during regular hours?"

"Too important, McCool," says Sullivan.

"OK, what is it?"

"Accessory to the utterance of an altered paint invoice."

"What?!"

"Accessory to the utterance of an altered paint invoice. You know—a forged paint invoice."

"You've got to be kidding. You come here at 5:30 and you want me to prosecute a forged paint invoice case?"

"Well, there's also distribution of cocaine," she says.

"Cocaine?"

"Yes. And," she adds, "I almost forgot. There's murder."

Using a microscope, a ballistics expert examines a bullet removed from a victim's body.

McCool looks up at Sullivan. Then he laughs. "OK, Sullivan. Do we really have a murder?"

"We're still waiting on ballistics, but here's what we've got." She explains the events of the last several days and describes the forensic evidence. "The DNA ties it all together," she continues. "DNA samples from under the victim's fingernails match on twelve points the DNA from hair found in the warehouse rest room. Fingerprints from the warehouse also match a print found at the crime scene. The name on the sign at the paint warehouse, Conroy Delman, matches the registration on the abandoned truck.

"Finally, the DNA from some of the hairs found at the warehouse matches the DNA from the skull we found in a cavern in Shenandoah County."

"Now wait!" McCool holds up his hands. "What's this about a skull?"

"We don't know what that means yet," says Sullivan. "I think we have two murders."

McCool is instantly all business. "Let's get an arrest warrant for Delman." He looks over at Vasquez. "Vasquez, throttle your partner for me, will you? She keeps pulling my chain. She thinks I'm too young to be a prosecutor."

Sullivan smiles and pats McCool on the back. "Come on, McCool, coffee's on me."

Ballistics is the branch of forensic science that deals with firearms and bullets. If you've watched detective shows on TV or read detective novels, then you know that a ballistics expert can match a bullet to the specific gun that fired it. This is possible because of the comparison microscope. With a comparison microscope, investigators can examine two bullets at the same time, side by side or with one bullet superimposed over the other. This makes it easy to compare the bullets' markings.

The comparison microscope is often used along with a helixometer. This is a thin, lighted scope that is inserted into the barrel of a gun. The inside of most gun barrels is rifled—that is, it has a series of spiral grooves cut into the metal. As a bullet is fired and speeds down the bore (hole) of the gun, the rifling causes the bullet to spin, much as a football spins when it is thrown properly.

Early guns had smooth barrels and fired round bullets. These guns did not shoot very far or very accurately. Around 1665, rifled guns were introduced in Europe and soon spread to the American colonies. Many types of modern firearms, including rifles, howitzers, pistols, and machine guns, have rifled barrels. Shotguns do not have rifled barrels.

With a helixometer, an investigator can examine the grooves of the rifling as well as the raised areas between the grooves, called lands. As a fired bullet speeds down a gun barrel, the spiral markings from the lands and grooves get etched into it. Because the arrangement of lands and grooves and the twist and angle of the spiraling differ slightly in every gun, it's possible to identify the type of gun that fired a bullet. Each gun also has unique scratches and other distinguishing marks that transfer to the bullet. Thus, investigators can match a bullet to the specific gun that fired it, whether the gun is a rifle or a pistol. (A rifle is a gun fired from the shoulder, while a pistol is a handgun.)

A bullet is basically a metal slug, usually made of lead. It fits snugly inside a metal casing, the cartridge, which contains a load of gunpowder and a charge (a small detonator cap). When the gun is fired, a firing pin is released and strikes the back of the cartridge. This ignites the detonator cap inside, causing the gunpowder to explode and propel the bullet out of the barrel.

If detectives find a bullet at a crime scene, the first thing they do is check the bullet's caliber. Caliber is simply a measurement of the opening of the gun barrel—its inner diameter. This diameter may be measured in inches or millimeters. A .38 caliber pistol has a gun barrel diameter of $^{38}/_{100}$ of an inch, or a little more than one-third of an inch. In a 9mm pistol, the gun barrel opening is 9 millimeters across.

In addition to checking the bullet's caliber, crime investigators count the lands and grooves and see whether they twist to the left or the right. This helps identify the type of weapon they are seeking. Some gun manufacturers build guns with left-twisting barrels, while others build them with right-twisting barrels.

When a firearm suspected of being used to commit a crime is brought to the laboratory, investigators first examine the barrel. When a gun is fired, a vacuum is created as the bullet leaves the barrel. The vacuum sucks air and lightweight materials near the gun into the barrel. This phenomenon, known as blowback, can draw clothing, fibers, hair, and even blood from a shooting victim into the gun barrel. These materials are carefully removed from the gun bore. They are examined under the microscope and undergo chemical analysis.

Next, investigators fire the gun so they will have a bullet for comparison with any bullets found at the crime scene. The standard technique is to fire two shots into a tank of water. The bullets slow down in the water, so they don't hit anything with full force. There is essentially no damage done to them, making comparisons easier.

Often a recovered bullet is so damaged from striking an object, such as the victim's bone or a wall, that the bullet cannot be analyzed in the usual way. But the smashed bullet probably

A police investigator fires a pistol to collect the spent bullet for comparison with a bullet found at a crime scene.

picked up microscopic particles that can be seen under the microscope. These particles tell their own story. Did the bullet strike the victim directly, or did it pass through another material first, such as a window or curtain? Did the bullet strike the victim by accident after ricocheting off a wall?

Suppose a bullet is recovered from a man's chest. The investigator finds that one side of the cone-shaped bullet has a small dent in it. Examination of the victim's chest reveals a nick in his rib. Comparing the damaged rib and the dent on the bullet confirms that the bullet glanced off the victim's rib before lodging in his chest. The investigator can estimate the line of

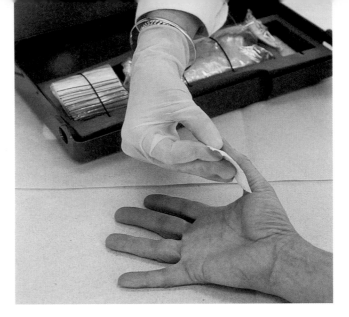

A technician searches for gunpowder on a suspected gunman's hand.

fire by calculating the angle from the entry wound to the point where the bullet struck a bone. This angle shows the position of the gun barrel when the weapon was fired. In some cases, the path a bullet traveled through the body can be seen on X rays or CAT scans.

Sometimes a bullet can be linked to a crime even if the gun is not found. If a gun is fired at close range, gunpowder often leaves a residue on the victim's skin or clothing. Gunpowder residue is sometimes found on a bullet as well. The gunpowder charge can often be identified and matched, because cartridges are loaded with charges in batches. The chemical composition of each batch differs.

THE CASE

In the laboratory, Sara Miner, the technician, wearing latex gloves, carefully removes the paint-coated .22 caliber pistol from the specimen bag and places it in an empty glass tank. First she sponges the excess paint away with a small amount of carbon tetrachloride, a solvent that dissolves materials such as paint. She is careful not to damage the gun while she wipes away the paint with soft cotton swabs. Particles picked up on the swabs will be analyzed in the lab. Miner lowers the gun into another tank, which is filled with luke-warm water and a mild, nonalkaline detergent. After allowing the gun to soak for several hours, the technician again wipes it with cotton swabs.

She does this second cleaning under a magnifying glass and bright fluorescent lamps. Using fine-tip forceps, she gently removes all fibers and other materials. As Miner works, she sees several fine strands of hair caught under the grip of the gun handle. She slowly removes them, puts them in glass collection tubes, and sends them to the chemistry lab for analysis.

When the weapon is clean, it is sent to the ballistics lab, where the gun is loaded and fired into a tank of water. With a compari-son microscope, the undamaged bullet is compared with the bullet recovered from Ann Marlboro's chest. They match. Both bullets are from the same gun.

Meanwhile, the strands of hair are analyzed using gas chro-matography and mass spectrometry. In addition to paint residues, the hair contains traces of hair dye similar to the dye found in hair samples taken from the victim at the autopsy. Microscopic exami-nation of the hair found on the gun and the victim's hair indicates a reasonable match.

Miner removes the handle grips from the gun and scrapes a brown material from inside one of them. DNA analysis shows that the brown material is decomposed blood from the victim.

Her phone call to Sullivan is brief. "This gun was not only the one fired into the victim," she says, "but is probably also the blunt instrument the murderer used to inflict the fatal blow."

SOLVING THE CRIME

THE *CASE*

On Friday, Sullivan and Vasquez travel to Charlottesville, 100 miles south of Fairfax. There, they meet with the chief of police and a handful of Charlottesville detectives. The plan is to capture the suspect and his drug contact at the same time.

At 1:30 P.M., five detectives, wearing sloppy street clothes, wander into Carol's Tea Room. Across the street sit two unmarked police cars containing more nonuniformed officers. Sullivan and Vasquez enter the tavern. The place is crowded and noisy.

The detectives work their way to the corner, where they can watch the door. The other three detectives find spots near the door. At two o'clock, they become alert. But there is no sign of their suspect.

As they wait, Vasquez notices a man in his late twenties with a crew cut and two earrings in his left ear who is looking constantly toward the door. In a few minutes, the young man smiles. Vasquez follows the man's gaze toward the other side of the room.

"In the corner," whispers Vasquez.

Sullivan turns. Conroy Delman has shaved his beard and cut his long scraggly hair, but the two detectives recognize his surly look. Sullivan signals the other detectives and they quickly grab Delman.

A skilled court reporter accurately records every word of a trial as it is spoken.

"You're under arrest," announces Sullivan.

The young man with the two earrings quickly turns, pushes a spectator aside, and darts toward an open window. Vasquez races after him. The young man stops at the window, turns, and pulls a gun from his pocket. "Hold it," he shouts. "Nobody move!"

Without breaking his stride, Vasquez kicks his right leg in a high arc. His foot strikes the young man's hand and the gun flies into the air. Turning to his right, Vasquez catches the gun in midair. "And you, too, are under arrest, buddy," he says.

"Read them their rights," says Sullivan as the police officers place the two men in handcuffs.

Then she turns to Vasquez. "That was fantastic. How did you learn to do that?"

Vasquez flashes a broad grin. "Soccer. Since childhood."

THE ARREST AND ARRAIGNMENT

There are three ways a suspect can be charged with a crime:

(1) A law enforcement officer has the authority to place a suspect under arrest by verbally telling him why he is being arrested. A suspect can be asked by the police to come to the station for questioning, but he cannot be forced to answer any questions until he has been advised of his rights under the Constitution of the United States. These rights include the right to remain silent, because any statement made can be used in court, and the right to have a lawyer. Reading a suspect his rights is often referred to as a Miranda warning.

(2) Based on an affidavit—a statement given under oath by a law enforcement officer, setting forth the criminal charges—an arrest warrant can be issued. Police then serve the warrant on the suspect and arrest him.

Once under arrest, an accused person is placed in handcuffs and taken to a police station to begin the judicial process.

(3) A grand jury, after reviewing evidence presented by the prosecuting attorney or based on its own investigation, can issue an indictment—a formal charge of a crime. After an indictment is issued, an arrest warrant is prepared and served to the suspect.

Once a suspect has been arrested, he is brought before a judge or magistrate in an arraignment. At an arraignment, the suspect, now referred to as the defendant, is read the charges against him and can enter a plea of guilty or not guilty. If he pleads guilty, a date will be set for sentencing. If he pleads not guilty, other court proceedings will be scheduled. The judge may set bond.

In setting bond, the judge decides what amount of money must be placed with the clerk of the court to guarantee that the suspect will show up in court for the next hearing. If the suspect appears on the appointed day, the bond is released (unless carried over to another hearing). If the suspect fails to appear, the bond is forfeited to the government, and the suspect is charged with an additional crime.

Often a citizen of good standing in the community will be "released on his own recognizance." This means that he takes an oath that he will appear in court when he is supposed to, and he will be trusted to do so. Sometimes the judge determines that a suspect is likely to be dangerous or to flee if released on bond. In such a case, the court can hold the suspect without bond, and the suspect must remain in jail until his trial.

A bond is usually many thousands of dollars. It can be paid in cash, but most often a fee is paid to a bail bondsman, who then "posts a bond"—guaranteeing to pay the bond amount if the suspect does not appear in court. When a suspect jumps bail and flees, he is hunted not only by the police, but also by private bounty hunters hired by the bail bondsman.

THE HEARING

In some states, a preliminary hearing follows the arraignment. At the preliminary hearing, the prosecuting attorney presents evidence to the judge to establish probable cause that the suspect committed the crime. If there is not enough evidence to establish probable cause, the suspect is immediately released. If there is enough evidence, the court (a judge or magistrate is often referred to as "the court") may issue an "information," a document that sets forth the formal charges. Alternately, the judicial officer may hold the suspect until the facts can be considered by a grand jury. In some states, the prosecuting attorney may submit these facts directly to a grand jury, without a preliminary hearing. In either case, the judicial officer will set bail or decide to deny bail.

Because of intense pressure to move more and more cases through the crowded criminal court system, roughly 90 percent of all criminal cases are resolved through a plea bargain. In a plea bargain, the defendant pleads guilty to charges agreed upon by the defendant and the prosecution. The terms of the plea bargain are prepared as a written agreement, which is signed by the accused person and the prosecuting attorney. Sometimes the bargain involves changing the number and nature of the criminal charges. Other times it involves only the prosecutor's recommendation for sentencing. The federal government and many states have rules that control how plea bargains are made.

Only ten percent of crimes actually result in a trial by jury. Most criminal cases are resolved by a plea bargain.

THE CASE

Sullivan and Vasquez sit at the back of a wood-paneled courtroom in the Fairfax County Courthouse. They are here to testify at the arraignment of Conroy Delman. The defendant, wearing a prisoner's orange jumpsuit, stands with his attorney in front of the judge and pleads "not guilty" as the charges are read. At the time, though, both he and his lawyer know that they are going to try to make a plea bargain, because the forensic evidence against Delman is so overwhelming.

As required by law, the prosecuting attorney, Daniel McCool, has informed Delman's lawyer of the evidence he has against Delman. The defense lawyer knows that if the case went to trial, all the material that was analyzed in the forensic laboratories would be presented to a jury. The forensic specialists whose work helped solve this crime would come into court as expert witnesses.

The lead detective, Detective Sullivan, would give the initial testimony, describing her investigation and the evidence she found. The medical examiner would discuss her findings from the autopsy, and other experts who performed various forensic tests would testify. In a trial, expert witnesses first describe their education and training so the judge can rule if they are qualified to give their opinion.

Delman's lawyer knows that in a trial, Delman would most likely be found guilty. Therefore, the lawyer makes it clear to the prosecutor that he will recommend a plea bargain for his client. He plans to have Delman plead guilty to second-degree murder (rather than to the more serious first-degree murder, which carries a mandatory life sentence) and bargain for a minimum sentence. If a bargain is reached, Delman will appear before the judge at a second hearing and change his plea from not guilty to guilty. Another hearing will be scheduled for sentencing.

After the arraignment, Delman and his lawyer meet with Sullivan, Vasquez, McCool, and a court reporter who will transcribe the meeting. The defendant knows that he has to tell all, including the names of those in the drug ring, or else the plea bargain will fall through and he'll have to stand trial.

"Start at the beginning," says Sullivan, leaning across the table toward Delman.

"You know everything," the defendant grumbles.

"Talk to us."

"Go ahead, Conroy," says his lawyer.

"I had a good deal going," he begins. "A really slick deal. But I should've known that if you tell a woman not to do something, she's gonna do it."

"What do you mean?" asks Vasquez.

"I told that Marlboro woman never to come to my warehouse. So what does she do? She comes to the warehouse and messes everything up." Delman waves his arms. "Our deal was that she would intercept small orders from a few new customers that her bosses would know nothin' about. Me and a couple guys would steal a few cans of paint here and there where nobody would notice and fill the orders. We'd split the profits with her—she gets 40 percent and I get 60. Of course, this was just to fool her, 'cause selling paint under a legitimate company name was a cover for our drug sales. But Marlboro, she didn't know nothin' about the drug money.

"Then one day she calls, all in a huff. She says she found an invoice to an outfit in Ruckersville that she hadn't supplied. She thinks I'm not sharing with her. So I try to calm her down. I say, 'Sure, I made a mistake. Of course I'm gonna give you your 40 percent of that $150 sale to Ruckersville.' But she still ain't happy. She says, 'I'm coming out to see what other deals you didn't cut me in on.' I warned her not to come out."

He shakes his head. "But she didn't listen. Next thing I know, she's messing around my warehouse. I find her in the office and I lead her out the door. Outside, I act a little rough to scare her. Then I say, 'Get out and don't come back.'"

"Then what?" asks Vasquez.

"I get to thinking, maybe that was dumb. So I go to her house. It's getting dark. She sees me and asks what I'm doing at her house.

"I say, 'I want that copy of the Ruckersville invoice and I want to know how you got it.'

"She says, 'None of your business.' She wanted to see all my records, said she was taking all the risk and could get in trouble.

"'Give me that invoice,' I says, and I flash my hunting knife at her. I wasn't going to use it. I just wanted to scare her. She says it's up in her bedroom. I follow her up the stairs. In the bedroom, she says, 'It's in the desk.' She goes to the desk, takes out the invoice, crushes it in her hand, and throws it at me. It falls to the floor. As I go to pick it up, she reaches back in the desk drawer and pulls out a gun.

"'Whoa,' I say and stop in my tracks.

"'Now get out of here,' she says.

"Then I pulled the oldest trick in the book." Delman flashes a broad grin. "I say, 'Charlie, grab that woman!' She turns and I stab her in the back. She turns back and I stab her again. She knocks the knife away, and I grab the gun out of her hand. She claws at me, so I hit her on the head with the gun. She falls straight down, and before I know what I'm doing, I stick the gun in her chest and shoot her dead."

He pauses, then says, "As soon as I seen what I done, I figure I'll be calm and smart like always. So I fix everything up, and I don't touch any of the blood, which is everywhere. Then I see she got mud on her shoes when she came to my warehouse, so I go in her closet and pick out a nice pair of shoes for her. I switch her shoes and take the dirty ones and the gun with me. Then I sneak out of the house.

"I didn't ever plan to kill her. She was gonna kill me and I was defending myself."

"What about Lo Ming Chow?"

"Oh, him."

"The owner of your building," says Sullivan.

"I didn't kill him. I don't know why he died. Over the years, he was always in the warehouse fussing about not gettin' his stupid rent money. The last time he came, he just fell over dead as road-kill. I figure it was a heart attack. In my situation, I couldn't have people coming around asking questions, so I buried him out in the back."

"But we found his skull in a cavern."

Delman laughs. "He'd been dead over a year when the rains from the hurricane swept in and washed old Lo Ming right up out of the ground. When I saw the skeleton, I took his bones and scattered them around an old cavern I knew about down in the mountains. I figured only kids went into that cave. Besides, they were just bones. Get the skin off and we all look alike, right?" He chuckles, but nobody smiles. "Who would know?"

"I think I've heard enough," says McCool to Delman's lawyer. "I want a list of everyone in the drug ring, then we'll discuss a plea."

As they walk out of the room, McCool says to Sullivan and Vasquez, "Great job, guys."

"Not just us," says Sullivan. "It was the gang in forensics. They made the objects talk."

GLOSSARY

analog equalizer: an instrument used to improve the sound on an audio recording or remove unwanted sounds by boosting or reducing sound frequencies (the number of sound waves that pass a fixed point per second)

antigen: any substance that causes an immune reaction in the body

arraignment: a court hearing at which a defendant (a person accused of committing a crime) is informed of the charges against him or her and can enter a plea of guilty or not guilty

aural analysis: studying spoken words

autopsy: the medical examination of a body after death to determine the cause of death

ballistics: a forensic science that deals with firearms and bullets

blood type: one of the four classes (A, B, AB, O) into which blood is grouped, based on the presence or absence of specific antigens; also called *blood group*

blowback: the sucking of air and lightweight materials into the barrel of a gun as it is fired, caused by a vacuum created when the bullet leaves the gun

chain of custody: a procedure for documenting who handles a piece of evidence in a criminal case

chromatograph: an instrument for performing chromatography, either with gas or liquid

chromatography: a process that separates materials into their basic molecular components

chromosomes: tightly coiled spools of DNA (deoxyribonucleic acid). The nucleus of each cell in the human body contains chromosomes. Half of an individual's forty-six chromosomes are inherited from each parent.

comparison microscope: a microscope made up of two compound microscopes with one combined viewing unit. The two microscopes focus on different points, allowing the viewer to see two objects at the same time side by side or superimposed over one another.

compound microscope: an optical instrument with two or more lenses that provides an enlarged view of an object

DNA (deoxyribonucleic acid): a molecule in the nuclei of cells that contains instructions determining the characteristics of organisms

DNA testing: extracting and examining DNA from body cells (the "DNA fingerprint") to identify an individual

electron microscope: a microscope that uses a flow of electrons to produce an image that is magnified up to one million times

electrostatic detection apparatus: a device used to discover invisible indentations on paper

exchange principle (or "theoretical exchange"): a theory, developed by Edmond Locard, stating that when two objects or people come in contact with each other, there is an exchange of material between them

exemplars: handwriting samples used in a court case to determine if a document contains a forgery

facial reconstruction: sketching a picture or creating a sculpture of a deceased person's head and face, based on the skull alone

fingerprint: an impression of the fingertips, marked by ridges that form patterns

fingerprinting: using ink to get an impression of the fingertip for identification purposes

forensic anthropology: the study of skeletal remains (bones) involved in crimes

forensic entomology: the study of insects as they relate to criminal investigations

forensic odontology: the study of teeth and teeth marks to identify a victim or suspect in a crime

forensic science: using the tools of scientific study in law enforcement and court cases

genes: segments of a DNA molecule that carry the genetic code, determining characteristics living things pass on to their offspring

genetic markers: enzymes and proteins in blood that differ from person to person and can be used for identification

helixometer: a thin, lighted scope that is inserted into the barrel of a gun to see its grooves and lands

indictment: a document stating the details of a crime with which a person is charged

infrared light: part of the light spectrum outside the visible spectrum, near the red end

mass spectrometer: a device used to determine the mass of the basic components of a sample material and identify the molecules

mass spectroscopy: firing a narrow beam of atoms or molecules into a magnetic field to determine the mass of each particle

microtraces: minute particles of material

nucleotides: chemical units that make up a DNA molecule. Nucleotides have three parts: a phosphate, a sugar, and a base.

pathology: the study of disease and disease processes

plea bargain: an agreement that is negotiated between a prosecutor and a defendant, in which the defendant agrees to plead guilty to lesser charges or in exchange for a lighter sentence

polarizing microscope: a microscope that uses a polarizing filter, or polarizer, which makes light waves vibrate in a specific direction rather than randomly in all directions as in ordinary light

questioned document: a paper or piece of writing involved in a crime

RNA (ribonucleic acid): a molecule in the nucleus of a cell that controls the cell's chemical activities

search warrant: an official paper issued by a judge or magistrate authorizing the police or other law enforcement officers to enter a specified place and conduct a search as defined in the warrant

serology: the science of blood testing

spectrogram: a visual image of a spectrum. A spectrum is a way of displaying information about a particular characteristic of a material.

spectroscopy: the production and analysis of spectra

stereomicroscope: also called stereoscopic microscope; it consists of two microscopes mounted side by side with a single viewer. The two microscopes are focused on the same point, providing a three-dimensional view of the object.

subpoena: a court order requiring someone to appear in court

toxicology: the study of poisons and drugs

ultraviolet light: part of the light spectrum outside the visible spectrum, near the violet end

waveform analysis: studying sound by using a visual presentation of the sound waves

FOR FURTHER READING

BOOKS

Camenson, Blythe. *Opportunities in Forensic Careers*. Chicago: VGM Career Books, 2001.

Casey, Eoghan. *Digital Evidence and Computer Crime: Forensic Science, Computers, and the Internet*. San Diego: Academic Press, 2000.

Delong, Candice, and Elisa Petrini. *Special Agent: My Life on the Front Lines as a Woman in the FBI*. New York: Hyperion, 2001.

Fisher, Barry A. J. *Techniques of Crime Scene Investigation*. Boca Raton, FL: CRC Press, 2000.

Goff, M. Lee, and Amy Bartlett Wright. *A Fly for the Prosecution: How Insect Evidence Helps Solve Crimes*. Cambridge, MA: Harvard University Press, 2000.

Huber, Roy A., and Alfred Headrick. *Handwriting Identification: Facts and Fundamentals*. Boca Raton, FL: CRC Press, 1999.

Nickell, Joe, and John F. Fischer. *Crime Science: Methods of Forensic Detection*. Lexington, KY: University Press of Kentucky, 1999.

Taylor, Karen T. *Forensic Art and Illustration*. Boca Raton, FL: CRC Press, 2001.

WEBSITES

<http://www.aafs.org>
Learn about careers in forensics and contact forensic scientists.

<http://www.mysterynet.com>
Find mystery books and movies and solve original crimes on your own.

INDEX

affidavit, 73, 106
analog equalizer, 81–82
arraignment, 107
arrests, 106–107
arrest warrant, 106–107
audio analysis, 80–82
aural analysis, 81
autopsy, 7, 31–39, 55;
    external examination,
    32–34; incisions, 34–35

bail, 108
ballistics, 98–103
Bandera, Marilyn, 93
blood, 10, 33, 39, 91, 93.
    See also forensic serology
bloodstain patterns, 16–19;
    computer program to
    analyze, 17; edge
    characteristics of, 16,
    20–21; point of
    convergence, 17
blowback, 100
blunt instruments, 18, 33,
    38, 103
body temperature, 32
bond, 107–108
bones, 10, 63; and
    determination of age,
    occupation, sex, race,
    and size, 64–68; joints,
    65
brain, 35
Brennan, William, 74
bromoform, 45
bullets. *See* ballistics

calcite, 57
caliber, 100
cameras. *See* photography
carbon tetrachloride, 103
cause of death, 35–36
chain of custody, 12–13

chemistry, 8–9, 19, 27, 41,
    55, 102–103
chromatography, 27, 55–56
civil court cases, 13
clothing, 32–33
Constitution of the United
    States, 106; Fourth
    Amendment, 74
coroner, 10
coroner's inquest, 10
court, the, 108
crime investigation team, 7
crime laboratories, 8, 27
crime scene, 7, 12, 86
criminal justice system, 10,
    109
criminal law, 13

defendant, 11, 107
defense lawyer, 110
detectives, homicide, 7, 10,
    12, 32, 86
Digital Signal Processing
    (DSP), 82
DNA (deoxyribonucleic
    acid), 89–91; analysis of,
    41, 82, 88, 91–93, 98
drugs and poisons, 10, 36,
    55

electrostatic detection
    apparatus, 26–27
entomologists, 10
evidence, 12–13, 74,
    76–77
exchange principle, 8–9
exemplars, 29

facial reconstruction, 68–69
Fast Fourier Transform
    Digital Noise Reduction
    (FFT/DNR), 82

Federal Bureau of
    Investigation (FBI), 38,
    45, 87, 93
fibers, 42
fingernails, scrapings under,
    8, 32, 34, 41
fingerprints, 7, 12, 23, 25,
    85–88
forensic, definition of, 7
forensic pathology, 9, 10
forensic scientists, 7–9, 13,
    44; anthropologists, 63;
    geologists, 55;
    hematologists, 10;
    odontologists, 66;
    psychiatrists, 10;
    toxicologists, 55, 57
forensic serology, 19
forgery, 26, 28
formalin, 35

gas chromatograph, 56,
    103
genetic markers, 19–20
glass, 43–44
gunpowder, 33, 102
guns, 33, 38. *See also*
    ballistics

hair, 18, 44, 103
handwriting, 25, 28–29
hemorrhage, 35

indictment, 11
ink, 26–27
Integrated Automated
    Fingerprint
    Identification System, 87
Iscan, Mehmet Yasar, 65

Jeffreys, Alec, 91
judges, 11, 12, 107–108
judicial officer, 11

juries, 11, 109

lasers, 86
lead, 41, 54
light: infrared, 28; ultraviolet (UV/Woods lamp), 19, 26
limestone. *See* calcite
Locard, Edmond, 8
Loth, Susan R., 65
Luminol, 19
Lyons Police Laboratory, 8

magistrates, 11
mass spectrometer, 56–57
medical examiner, 7, 10, 31–32, 55, 110
microscopes, 8, 25, 29, 66; comparison, 98–99; types of, 46–47
microtraces. *See* particles
Miranda warning, 106
morgue, 7, 32

No More Strings, 17

oil, 54–55

paint, 44
paper, 25–27
particles, 8–9, 32–33, 72, 101; collecting, 42
pathologists, 10
pelvic bones, 64–65
photography, 18, 26, 32, 66
plea bargains, 109–111
preliminary hearings, 108–109
probable cause, 74, 77
prosecuting (district) attorney, 11, 12, 108–110

questioned documents, 25

Reaves III, Mack, 93

refractive index, 44
RNA (ribonucleic acid), 90–91

search warrants, 73–75, 77
skeleton. *See* bones
skull, 65, 69. *See also* bones
soil, 44–45
sound, 81
spectroscopy, 8, 55, 57
stalagmites and stalactites, 58
subpoena, 11

teeth, 10, 63–67
totality of the circumstances, 74–75
toxicology, 55, 57

ultrasonic cleaner, 45
U.S. Supreme Court, 74

waveform analysis, 81
wounds, 33, 35

ABOUT THE AUTHORS

Mark P. Friedlander Jr. has been a trial attorney in Washington, D.C., and northern Virginia for over forty years. He is the author of several books, including *Outbreak: Disease Detectives at Work,* and he coauthored *The Immune System* with Terry M. Phillips. Both books are part of the Discovery! series.

Terry M. Phillips, an immunologist for more than twenty years, founded the Analytical Immunochemistry Laboratories at George Washington Medical Center in Washington, D.C., and is chief of the Ultramicro Analytical Immunochemistry Resource at the National Institutes of Health in Bethesda, Maryland. He has aided courts in forensic matters. In his professional career, he has collaborated with investigators in Europe, Canada, and Japan, as well as the United States, and he has authored more than 250 scientific articles and several books.

PHOTO ACKNOWLEDGMENTS

The photographs in this book are reproduced courtesy of: Peter Arnold, Inc.: (© Volker Steger) pp. 1, 33, (© Michel Viard) pp. 21, 34, 70, 96, 101, 102, (© Robert Holmgren) p. 28, (© Dr. Stanley L. Gibbs) p. 66, (© Martha Cooper) p. 76; © Richard Nowitz, pp. 2-3; © Tom and Therisa Stack/Tom Stack and Associates, p. 6; **Photo Researchers, Inc.:** (© Kenneth Murray) p. 9, (© Mark C. Burnett) p. 22, (© SCIMAT 1999) p. 27, (© Dr. Jurgen Scriba/Science Photo Library) pp. 40, 45, (© Andrew Syred/Science Photo Library) p. 43, (© Dr. Tony Brain/Science Photo Library) p. 46, (© Biophoto Associates) p. 52, (© Colin Cuthbert/Science Photo Library) p. 56, (© Nancy J. Pierce) p. 60, (© VideoSurgery) p. 64, (© Nancy J. Pierce/Science Source) p. 68, (© Hank Morgan/Science Source) p. 78, (© Gontier P) p. 83, (© Simon Fraser/Science Photo Library) p. 84, (© James King-Holmes/Science Photo Library) p. 87, (© Kenneth Eward/Science Source) p. 89, (© B. Seitz) p. 104, (© David R. Frazier Photolibrary) pp. 107, 109; © Norman Reeves, pp. 14, 17; © Australian Picture Library/CORBIS, p. 30; © A. J. Copley/Visuals Unlimited, p. 58; © Reuters NewMedia Inc./CORBIS, p. 75; © Richard T. Nowitz/CORBIS, p. 92.

Front cover: © Manfred Kaoe/Peter Arnold, Inc. (top left), © Tom and Therisa Stack/Tom Stack and Associates (center), Dan Mahoney/IPS (bottom left), © Voker Steger/Peter Arnold, Inc. (bottom right).